An Unexpected Journal

The Genius of G.K. Chesterson

Advent 2019

Volume 2, Issue 4

Credits
Managing Editor: Zak Schmoll
Cover Art: Virginia De La Lastra
Journal Mark: Erica McMillan
Journal Design and Layout: Legacy Marketing Services
Editors: Carla Alvarez, Donald W. Catchings, Jr., Annie Crawford, Jason Monroe, Annie Nardone, Zak Schmoll, Rebekah Valerius
Contributors: Nancy Carpenter Brown, Donald W. Catchings, Jr., G.K. Chesterton, Mark Linville, Seth Myers, Joseph Pearce, Zak Schmoll, Melissa Cain Travis, Rebekah Valerius, Michael Ward, Clark Weidner, Shawn White

An Unexpected Journal
Houston, TX

http://anunexpectedjournal.com
Email: anunexpectedjournal@gmail.com

CONTENTS

Literary Priests in the Tavern at the End of the World...5
Joseph Pearce

Chesterton as Storyteller: The Shop of Ghosts 11
G.K. Chesterton from *Tremendous Trifles*

Chesterton and the Seven Heavens 21
Michael Ward

The White Light of Wonder: G.K. Chesterton's Philosophy of Art 49
Melissa Cain Travis

The Happy Home to Which We are All Faring......75
Rebekah Valerius

A "Defence" of Armchair Philosophy 95
Mark Linville

Chesterton as Philosopher: The Revival of Philosophy 131
G.K. Chesterton

Another Resurrection: If Only We Could Understand 143
Donald W. Catchings, Jr.

Creation, Corruption, and Celebration on a Thursday...151
Shawn White

Escaping the Madhouse 167
Clark Weidner

The Freedom of Boundaries.................................181
Zak Schmoll

Chesterton at the Movies 195
  Seth Myers

Frances Chesterton and Christmas 225
  Nancy Carpenter Brown

Chesterton as Poet: The Wise Men 233
  G.K. Chesterton

Resources... 237

To Connect with An Unexpected Journal 237

To Read More.. 238

Subscribe 238

About An Unexpected Journal............................. 239

Our Contributors 241

Thoughts from a Fellow Traveler 247
  By Jack Tollers

LITERARY PRIESTS IN THE TAVERN AT THE END OF THE WORLD

Joseph Pearce

All roads point at last to an ultimate inn, where we shall meet Dickens and all his characters: and when we drink again it shall be from the great flagons in the tavern at the end of the world.

G. K. Chesterton[1]

One wonders what Chesterton's Father Brown and Graham Greene's whisky priest would say to each other were they to meet in Chesterton's fantastic tavern at the world's end. What would these two unforgettable individuals, who would appear to have absolutely nothing in common except their priesthood, say to each other? What

---

[1] G. K. Chesterton, *Charles Dickens*, (London: Methuen & Co. Ltd., 15th edn., 1925) 212.

would we see and hear if we were flies on the wall at such a meeting? Perhaps we would see the whisky priest sitting disconsolately over his flagon of ale, wishing that he could exchange it for a bottle of cheap Kentucky bourbon. Looking up, his tired, bloodshot eyes might meet those of Father Brown. "You know," he mumbles, "we are more inclined to regret our virtues than our vices, but only the most honest will admit this."[2] Father Brown might place his own tankard on the table between them, his gratitude for the foam flecked nectar reinforcing a profound sense that he is unworthy of the gift he is imbibing. In the presence of such undeserved blessings, the whisky priest's words seem almost blasphemous. "I don't regret any virtues except those I have lost," mutters Father Brown. His thoughts are at least as sad as those of the whisky priest, but his sadness is of a very different sort. His is the sadness of humility, the sorrow that leads to contrition; the whisky priest's is the sadness of pride, the sadness of Milton's Satan whose greatest

---

[2] These words were actually written by Holbrook Jackson in his *Platitudes in the Making* (1911); Father Brown's reply to the whisky priest is actually Chesterton's riposte to Jackson. See Joseph Pearce, *Wisdom and Innocence: A Life of G. K. Chesterton*, London: Hodder & Stoughton, 1996, 173

sorrow is that he cannot escape from himself: "Which way I fly is Hell; myself am Hell."[3]

The abyss between these two types of sadness is as wide as the chasm that separates the inferno from paradise. Never the twain shall meet. But this begs an unsettling question: If the sorrow of the whisky priest is akin to the sadness of Satan, does this mean that the whisky priest belongs in hell? Heaven forbid; or heaven forbid, at least, that we should ever have the pride and audacity to place him there. His near heroic death and grudging acts of self-sacrifice might be said to have snatched him from Satan's grasp, and the reader is surely meant to give him the benefit of the doubt. Nonetheless, one can't help feeling irritated by the whisky priest's unrelenting joylessness, which is as unbelievable in a work of fiction as it is in the world of fact. The witness of real-life martyred priests, such as St. Edmund Campion and St. Robert Southwell, illustrate and illuminate the joy-filled courage with which these real men of faith met their martyrdom. A cursory perusal of Campion's famous "Brag" or Southwell's glorious poetry disperses the acrid aroma with which Greene surrounds his fictional martyr.

---

[3] John Milton, *Paradise Lost*, 4.75

Let's leave the whisky priest in the company of Father Brown, his literary and priestly antidote, and let's fly to another part of Chesterton's apocalyptic tavern. Passing over Chesterton himself, deep in conversation with Dickens amidst the motley company of the latter's fictional characters, we might alight on the ceiling above another gathering of literary priests. There we might see the impeccably spoken Jesuit, Father Mowbray, conversing convivially with the gritty Glaswegian, Father Mackay. Perhaps their discussion centres on the flightiness of the Flytes as they revisit Brideshead, reminiscing about their respective roles in the novel in which Waugh had placed them.

Flying on a little further, we come across Father Elijah discussing apocalyptic intrigues with several priests from the fiction of Robert Hugh Benson. At the next table, Biersach's Father Baptist confers with Father Luke Scott, from Piers Paul Read's *Death of a Pope*, about the dangers of modernism and liberation theology. Standing at the bar, a large group of men in Elizabethan garb are laughing heartily. Amongst them is the fictional martyr, Father Robin Audrey, from Benson's *Come Rack! Come Rope!*, but the others are real historical figures, including the aforementioned Campion and Southwell, along with a host of other jovial English

Martyrs. The joviality increases as Father Brown joins the company having just heard the whisky priest's confession.

At this point, our vision fades. It was, after all, only a dream, albeit a dream inspired by the imagination of G. K. Chesterton, who was very much awake when he imagined or "dreamed" it. Such dreams, in some manner or form, may come true but not presumably in every detail. It is, for instance, hardly likely that there would be any flies on the wall of such a heavenly tavern! If we were ever admitted to such a tavern we would presumably have to join the conversation like everyone else and not seek to become entomological eavesdroppers.

Having descended to earth with an unceremonious bump, our thoughts fall and falter from the heavenly sphere of the poetic to the mundane worldliness of the prosaic; settling finally on the level of the banal. We are reminded, for instance, that literary priests are like library books, which is to say that they can be categorized as fiction or non-fiction. Having taken our fictional flight of fancy with the fictional priests, we should not omit to mention those non-fictional priests who have given us such good literature. In our heavenly tavern, mingling with the fictional guests, we would surely find John Henry Newman and Gerard Manley Hopkins; Robert Hugh Benson and Ronald Knox.

Since there are no flies in such a tavern, and since we are not able to fly there ourselves, we will have to see Chesterton's tavern through the same eyes that he saw it; through the visionary eyes of the imagination. These are the eyes through which Chesterton first saw Father Brown and through which Michael D. O'Brien first saw Father Elijah. These are the eyes through which we also see these literary priests, and through which we see the deep truths that they convey to us. Like their non-fictional counterparts, these literary priests are ministers of grace blessing us with their sanctity and sagacity. Thank God for such blessings.

Chesterton as Storyteller: The Shop of Ghosts

G.K. Chesterton from *Tremendous Trifles*

Nearly all the best and most precious things in the universe you can get for a halfpenny. I make an exception, of course, of the sun, the moon, the earth, people, stars, thunderstorms, and such trifles. You can get them for nothing. Also, I make an exception of another thing, which I am not allowed to mention in this paper, and of which the lowest price is a penny halfpenny. But the general principle will be at once apparent. In the street behind me, for instance, you can now get a ride on an electric tram for a halfpenny. To be on an electric tram is to be on a flying castle in a fairy tale. You can get quite a large number of brightly coloured sweets for a halfpenny. Also, you can get the chance of reading this article for a halfpenny; along, of course, with other and irrelevant matter.

But if you want to see what a vast and bewildering array of valuable things you can get at a halfpenny each you should do as I was doing last night. I was gluing my nose against the glass of a very small and dimly lit toy shop in one of the greyest and leanest of the streets of Battersea. But dim as was that square of light, it was filled (as a child once said to me) with all the colours God ever made. Those toys of the poor were like the children who buy them; they were all dirty; but they were all bright. For my part, I think brightness more important than cleanliness; since the first is of the soul, and the second of the body. You must excuse me; I am a democrat; I know I am out of fashion in the modern world.

As I looked at that palace of pigmy wonders, at small green omnibuses, at small blue elephants, at small black dolls, and small red Noah's arks, I must have fallen into some sort of unnatural trance. That lit shop-window became like the brilliantly lit stage when one is watching some highly coloured comedy. I forgot the grey houses and the grimy people behind me as one forgets the dark galleries and the dim crowds at a theatre. It seemed as if the little objects behind the glass were small, not because they were toys, but because they were objects far away. The green omnibus was really a green omnibus, a green Bayswater omnibus, passing across some huge desert on its ordinary way to Bayswater. The blue elephant was no longer blue with paint; he was blue with distance. The black doll was really a negro relieved against passionate tropic foliage in the land where every weed is flaming and only man is black. The red Noah's ark was really the enormous ship of earthly salvation riding on the rain-swollen sea, red in the first morning of hope.

Every one, I suppose, knows such stunning instants of abstraction, such brilliant blanks in the mind. In such moments one can see the face of one's own best friend as an unmeaning pattern of spectacles or moustaches. They are commonly marked by the two signs of the slowness of their growth and the suddenness of their termination. The return to real thinking is often as abrupt as bumping into a man. Very often indeed (in my case) it is bumping into a man. But in any case the awakening is always emphatic and, generally speaking, it is always complete. Now, in this case, I did come back with a shock of sanity to the consciousness that I was, after all, only staring into a dingy little toy-shop; but in some strange way the mental cure did not seem to be final. There was still in my mind an unmanageable something that told me that I had strayed into some odd atmosphere, or that I had already done some odd thing. I felt as if I had worked a miracle or committed a sin. It was as if I had at any rate, stepped across some border in the soul.

To shake off this dangerous and dreamy sense I went into the shop and tried to buy wooden soldiers. The man in the shop was very old and broken, with confused white hair covering his head and half his face, hair so startlingly white that it looked almost artificial. Yet though he was senile and even sick, there was nothing of suffering in his eyes; he looked rather as if he were gradually falling asleep in a not unkindly decay. He gave me the wooden soldiers, but when I put down the money he did not at first seem to see it; then he blinked at it feebly, and then he pushed it feebly away.

"No, no," he said vaguely. "I never have. I never have. We are rather old-fashioned here."

"Not taking money," I replied, "seems to me more like an uncommonly new fashion than an old one."

"I never have," said the old man, blinking and blowing his nose; "I've always given presents. I'm too old to stop."

"Good heavens!" I said. "What can you mean? Why, you might be Father Christmas."

"I am Father Christmas," he said apologetically, and blew his nose again.

The lamps could not have been lighted yet in the street outside. At any rate, I could see nothing against the darkness but the shining shop-window. There were no sounds of steps or voices in the street; I might have strayed into some new and sunless world. But something had cut the chords of common sense, and I could not feel even surprise except sleepily. Something made me say, "You look ill, Father Christmas."

"I am dying," he said.

I did not speak, and it was he who spoke again.

"All the new people have left my shop. I cannot understand it. They seem to object to me on such curious and inconsistent sort of grounds, these scientific men, and these innovators. They say that I give people superstitions and make them too visionary; they say I give people sausages and make them too coarse. They say my heavenly parts are too heavenly; they say my earthly parts are too earthly; I don't know what they want, I'm sure. How can heavenly things be too heavenly, or earthly things too earthly? How can one be too good, or too jolly? I don't understand. But I understand one thing well enough. These modern people are living and I am dead."

"You may be dead," I replied. "You ought to know. But as for what they are doing, do not call it living.

A silence fell suddenly between us which I somehow expected to be unbroken. But it had not fallen for more than a few seconds when, in the utter stillness, I distinctly heard a very rapid step coming nearer and nearer along the street. The next moment a figure flung itself into the shop and stood framed in the doorway. He wore a large white hat tilted back as if in impatience; he had tight black old-fashioned pantaloons, a gaudy old-fashioned stock and waistcoat, and an old fantastic coat. He had large, wide-open, luminous eyes like those of an arresting actor; he had a pale, nervous face, and a fringe of beard. He took in the shop and the old man in a look that seemed literally a flash and uttered the exclamation of a man utterly staggered.

"Good lord!" he cried out; "it can't be you! It isn't you! I came to ask where your grave was."

"I'm not dead yet, Mr. Dickens," said the old gentleman, with a feeble smile; "but I'm dying," he hastened to add reassuringly.

"But, dash it all, you were dying in my time," said Mr. Charles Dickens with animation; "and you don't look a day older."

"I've felt like this for a long time," said Father Christmas.

Mr. Dickens turned his back and put his head out of the door into the darkness.

"Dick," he roared at the top of his voice; "he's still alive."

Another shadow darkened the doorway, and a much larger and more full-blooded gentleman in an enormous periwig came in, fanning his flushed face with a military hat of the cut of Queen Anne. He carried his head well back like a soldier, and his hot face had even a look of arrogance, which was suddenly contradicted by his eyes, which were literally as humble as a dog's. His sword made a great clatter, as if the shop were too small for it.

"Indeed," said Sir Richard Steele, "'tis a most prodigious matter, for the man was dying when I wrote about Sir Roger de Coverley and his Christmas Day."

My senses were growing dimmer and the room darker. It seemed to be filled with newcomers.

"It hath ever been understood," said a burly man, who carried his head humorously and obstinately a little on one side—I think he was Ben Jonson—"It hath ever been understood, consule Jacobo, under our King James and her late Majesty, that such good and hearty customs were fallen sick, and like to pass from the world. This grey beard most surely was no lustier when I knew him than now."

And I also thought I heard a green-clad man, like Robin Hood, say in some mixed Norman French, "But I saw the man dying."

"I have felt like this a long time," said Father Christmas, in his feeble way again.

Mr. Charles Dickens suddenly leant across to him.

"Since when?" he asked. "Since you were born?"

"Yes," said the old man, and sank shaking into a chair. "I have been always dying."

Mr. Dickens took off his hat with a flourish like a man calling a mob to rise.

"I understand it now," he cried, "you will never die."

Dr. Michael Ward in Chestertonian attire.

CHESTERTON AND THE SEVEN HEAVENS

Michael Ward

When discussing what he calls "The Fear of the Past"[1], Chesterton notes how we are so in love with progress that we are afraid of ever retracing our steps in case we should be accused of being old-fashioned. He observes that people are fond of saying, "You can't put the clock back" with regard to a certain piece of supposed progress, when a clock can, in fact, rather easily be put back and to do so is often the quickest way of correcting an error in time-keeping. Again, he points out how people are fond of remarking that once you have made your bed you have to lie in it. This isn't so; a bed can be remade, and if you have made an uncomfortable bed, it is only common sense to make it again.

Chesterton goes on: "We could restore the Heptarchy . . . if we chose. It might take some time to

G. K. Chesterton, "What's Wrong with the World," Project Gutenberg, accessed November 28, 2019, https://www.gutenberg.org/files/1717/1717-h/1717-h.htm.

do, and it might be very inadvisable to do it; but certainly it is not impossible as bringing back last Friday is impossible."

The heptarchy is another word for what the poet John Donne referred to as "the seven kingdoms of the seven planets."[2] In this essay I will address Chesterton's interest in that heptarchical, pre-Copernican, geocentric model of the cosmos and discuss his thoughts about the difficulty of living imaginatively in the post-Copernican, heliocentric cosmos.

A Brief History of the Heptarchy

Until the sixteenth century it was believed that there were only seven planets and that they occupied certain 'spheres' or 'heavens' from where they would shed influences upon Earth, affecting people, events, and even the metals in Earth's crust.

Earth was thought to be stationary and the centre of everything. Around this static and central Earth revolved these seven planets in their seven heavens. Working outwards from Earth, the order was as follows: Luna (the Moon), Mercury, Venus, Sol (the Sun), Mars, Jupiter, Saturn. These celestial bodies described their own peculiar paths across the

---

[2] John Donne, *Donne's Sermons* (Oxford: Clarendon Press, 1919), 160.

sky, which is why they were called *planets*, not *stars*. (The Greek word for 'wanderers' is *planetai*; a *planet* is a wandering star.) The fixed stars, in their constellations, were thought to occupy their own sphere called the Stellatum.

And this was not superstition or ignorance talking. The best minds of the day believed this to be a factual representation of reality. But then, in 1543, the Polish astronomer, Nicolaus Copernicus, published his epoch-making work *De Revolutionibus Orbium Coelestium* (*On the Revolutions of the Heavenly Spheres*), in which he theorized that we live not in a geocentric, but in a heliocentric universe. It was a theory that was later proved correct by Kepler and Galileo, aided by the invention of the telescope early in the seventeenth century.

The Copernican revolution has a good claim to being the most important change that there has ever been in the history of human thought because it gave our home, Earth – or *Planet* Earth, as it was now known – a new address in the universe. We no longer occupied the central place; rather, we were on the periphery and the Sun was at the centre.

However, the Copernican revolution, for all its hugeness in the annals of science, has not had quite so huge an effect upon human imagination as might have been supposed. In his 1901 collection of essays called *The Defendant*, Chesterton has a chapter entitled "A Defence of Planets", in which he confesses:

> It is a very remarkable thing that none of us are really Copernicans in our actual outlook upon things. We are convinced intellectually that we inhabit a small provincial planet, but we do not feel in the least suburban . . . If a single poem or a single story were really transfused with the Copernican idea, the thing would be a nightmare. Can we think of a solemn scene of mountain stillness in which some prophet is standing in a trance, and then realize that the whole scene is whizzing round like a zoetrope at the rate of nineteen miles a second? . . . A strange fable might be written of a man who was blessed or cursed with the Copernican eye, and saw all men on the earth like tintacks clustering round a magnet. It would be singular to imagine how very different the speech of an aggressive egoist, announcing the independence and divinity of man, would sound if he were seen hanging on to the planet by his boot soles . . . It would be an interesting speculation to imagine whether the world will ever develop a Copernican poetry and a Copernican habit of fancy; whether we shall ever speak of 'early earth-turn'

instead of 'early sunrise,' and speak indifferently of looking up at the daisies, or looking down on the stars.[3]

Chesterton's view is that the Copernican revolution has left the normal human imagination almost entirely unaffected; we can't ordinarily picture the reality of our situation in heliocentric terms for it is really too ridiculous. The sun really does seem to go across the sky; it really does seem as if the sun is moving and we are staying still. As the psalmist proclaims:

In [the heaven] hath God set a tabernacle for the sun,

which is as a bridegroom coming out of his chamber,

and rejoiceth as a strong man to run a race.

His going forth is from the end of the heaven,

and his circuit unto the ends of it:

---

[3] A Defence of Planets," in *The Defendant*, Project Gutenberg, accessed November 27, 2019, http://www.gutenberg.org/files/12245/12245-h/12245-h.htm

and there is nothing hid from the heat thereof.[4]

But however much we try to hammer into our brains the fact that the Sun does not actually move across the sky, that it is only a trick of perspective, the notion will not stick. Unlike Joshua (Josh. 10:12-14), we cannot make the sun stand still. Our minds and imaginations seem to be so configured – let us say, so created – that the sun seems to dote upon our little planet, caressing it all round every day. It is almost as if God loves us more than we love Him. We have good reason to believe that Earth is revolving round the Sun, like a moth fluttering round a candle flame, but it seems, for the life of us, as if it's entirely the other way round. Reality and appearance are here out of kilter. The universe is for a fact heliocentric. We experience it geocentrically.

Note in particular how Chesterton says, "If a . . . story were really transfused with the Copernican idea, the thing would be *a nightmare*." I shall be coming back to that below. For now let us return to the heptarchy and Chesterton's claims that "We could restore the Heptarchy . . . if we chose."[5]

---

[4] Psalm 19: 4b-6

[5] There is a small possibility that he was referring to a different heptarchy, the sevenfold division of ancient England into the seven kingdoms of Mercia, Northumbria, East Anglia, Kent, Essex, Sussex,

And we could indeed restore the planetary heptarchy. Chesterton is not suggesting that it would be *advisable* to restore it, that it would make good sense to overthrow all of the advances made by post-Copernican science, but only that, in theory at least, we could decide to live again in the pre-Copernican universe. We could shut our eyes to the last four hundred and fifty years of intellectual progress if we believed that science had led us not on a progression but a digression. We don't absolutely need to lie in the bed that we have made.

Chesterton raises this possibility not because he is a Luddite or obscurantist. He is merely wanting to interrogate certain assumptions about the world, to keep our unspoken presuppositions under constant surveillance and to ask questions of scientific progress in order to keep us on our toes, as it were, – to keep us alert to the way that purely scientific accounts of human experience do not, indeed cannot, give us a completely satisfying explanation of reality.

For part of our reality is that the earth does seem to be static and central; the sun truly does appear,

---

and Wessex. But he doesn't specify and so I assume that he means the planetary heptarchy, as that seems vastly more likely given his keen interest in cosmology.

from our point of view, to move across the sky. And that misleading appearance is itself a fact which doesn't fit easily within the categories of empirical science. A scientific account would simply tell us that our minds are mistaken and that the data are otherwise than we perceive them to be. Ah yes, but why do we perceive them to be this way? What does that perception itself tell us about ourselves, the universe, and the way the Creator has placed us in the universe? That is a theological question, or at the very least a psychological question: it is not a question that falls within the domain of the physical sciences.

Not only do we all still speak as if the Sun is going round the Earth, there is also another sense in which we still live in a pre-Copernican universe, for we still operate according to a seven-day week, and the names of the days of the week are themselves derived from this heptarchical system. We are in fact referring to this old view of the cosmos every day of our lives. Saturday is named after Saturn, Sunday after the Sun, Monday after the Moon, and so on.[6] In one way, therefore, we cannot restore the

---

[6] In the English language, for some reason lost in the mists of time, the other four days of the week are known by the names of the Norse deities, not the Roman ones. Tuesday comes from Tiw or Tyr, the Norse equivalent of Mars (think *Mardi* in French or *Martes* in Spanish); Wednesday from Woden, the Norse equivalent of Mercury

heptarchy, because we have never left it; it structures every single day of our lives, if calendrical nomenclature is any guide. And in Chesterton's case, so firmly fixed was the heptarchy within the furniture of his mind that, on the day he became engaged to be married (21 July 1898), he wrote to his fiancée, "Dearest Frances . . . it is no exaggeration to say that I never saw you in my life without thinking that I underrated you the time before. But today was something more than usual: you went up seven heavens at a run."

That concludes my brief history of the heptarchy. Now let us turn to consider the use that Chesterton made of the heptarchy in his writings.

What use did Chesterton make of the heptarchy?

The seven heavens are mentioned in at least four of Chesterton's poems ('Wine and Water', 'After Reading a Book of Modern Verse', 'Lost', 'To St Michael in Time of Peace'). In *The Everlasting Man* he writes that Christianity "had among other things a singular air of piling tower upon tower by the use of the *a fortiori*; making a pagoda of degrees like the

---

(*Mercredi, Miercoles*); Thursday from Thor, the Norse equivalent of Jove/Jupiter (*Jeudi, Jueves*); and Friday from Freya or Frigg, the Norse equivalent of Venus (*Vendredi, Viernes*).

seven heavens."[7] But by far the most important appearance of the heptarchy in his writings is in *The Man Who Was Thursday* – regarded by many as his greatest work of fiction; first published in 1908, it has never been out of print. How does Chesterton use the heptarchy in this novel?

As indicated in the very title, Chesterton is concerned with the days of the week. The protagonist, Gabriel Syme, is a man called 'Thursday' because he is a member of 'the Council of the Seven Days', also known as the Central European Council of Anarchists. The full Council is comprised of the following characters:

Sunday – The President of the Council, a huge, unsleeping man with a vast head

Monday – The Secretary of the Council, thin-faced and with a twisted smile

Tuesday – Gogol, a gloomy and hairy Pole

Wednesday – Inspector Ratcliffe, square bearded, frock-coated

Thursday – Gabriel Syme, the eponymous hero

Friday – Professor de Worms, senile and apparently moribund

---

[7] G. K. Chesterton, *The Everlasting Man*, Project Gutenberg Australia, accessed November 28, 2019, http://gutenberg.net.au/ebooks01/0100311.txt.

Saturday – Dr Bull, sphinx-like, black-haired, bespectacled

Chesterton introduces the characters into the story in no particular order, but towards the end of the story he shows himself to be aware of the traditional order of the planets when the Council members gather together for the grand denouement. They meet in a garden where, "in a kind of crescent, stood seven great chairs, the thrones of the seven days . . . but the central chair was empty."[8]

The central chair is the seat of Sunday, the President of the Council. But does this mean that the model of the cosmos that is on display in *The Man Who Was Thursday* is the post-Copernican, heliocentric model? It does not. For, somewhat confusingly, according to the *pre*-Copernican model, the Sun had a central position even though it was not completely and utterly central. The Sun was the central *planet*, fourth from the top and fourth from the bottom: Mars, Jupiter and Saturn rotated above the Sun; Venus, Mercury and Luna rotated below the Sun. This central position was held, in medieval

---

[8] G. K. Chesterton, *The Man Who Was Thursday*, Project Gutenberg, accessed November 27, 2019, https://www.gutenberg.org/files/1695/1695-h/1695-h.htm.

thought, to betoken a peculiar dignity or honour, like the heart in the middle of the body, or like a king surrounded by his subjects. The Sun is "the eye and mind of the whole universe" as C.S. Lewis wrote in his chapter on 'The Heavens' in *The Discarded Image*, and when Chesterton leaves the central chair empty for Sunday to sit in, he is acknowledging the centrality of the Sun within the heptarchical system. Yet although the Sun occupied this middle position among the seven planets, Earth was the very center of the whole universe, the focal point about which all the planets, including the Sun, revolved.

If this apparent clash of centers provokes a vague sense of discomfort in the reader, that is no doubt intentional on Chesterton's part. And at this point, we would do well to recall that *The Man Who was Thursday* has a subtitle. In an article published in *The Illustrated London News* on 13 June 1936, the day before his death, Chesterton drew attention to the very fact of this subtitle:

> The book was called *The Man Who was Thursday: A Nightmare* ... It was intended to describe the world of wild doubt and despair which the pessimists were generally describing at that date; with just a gleam of hope in some double meaning

of the doubt, which even the pessimists felt in some fitful fashion.[9]

This is a very helpful comment from the author. *The Man Who Was Thursday* is a nightmare story, but it contains a glimmer of a good dream in it somewhere. Let us refer again to what Chesterton said in his 'Defence of Planets' where he wrote, "If a . . . story were really transfused with the Copernican idea, the thing would be a nightmare." Is it possible that Chesterton subtitled *The Man Who Was Thursday* 'A Nightmare' because he wished to express the nightmarishly unstable quality of trying to live consciously in the Copernican cosmos? I think it is.

The Copernican idea is that we go round the Sun, and that is precisely what the man who is Thursday does in this novel, along with the men who are Monday, Tuesday, Wednesday, Friday and Saturday. They all go round the man who is Sunday: they revolve around the President of the Council. They are described in one place as his "satellites." He is the candle around which these moths flutter. More than once, the six other characters are called

---

[9] G. K. Chesterton, *The Man Who Was Thursday* (San Francisco: Ignatius Press, 2004), 281.

"wanderers," for they are the *planetai* in this Copernican system. Sunday is the cynosure who dominates both the Council of Anarchists and the police force: he is the figure in the dark room sitting with his back to the policemen as they each come in one by one to receive their orders.

The very first line of the novel indicates the centrality of the Sun: "The suburb of Saffron Park lay on the sunset side of London, as red and ragged as a cloud of sunset."[10] Twice in that sentence the word "sunset" appears, setting the keynote for the whole book: we are to be preoccupied with the sun, the sun at its setting. Later in that opening chapter we're told: "This particular evening, if it is remembered for nothing else, will be remembered in that place for its strange sunset . . . The very empyrean seemed to be a secret."[11] The sky this evening is "that impossible sky".

Once Gabriel Syme has joined the Central Council of Anarchists and become known as Thursday, things become even more impossible:

> [Syme] had a singular sensation of stepping out into something entirely new; not merely into the landscape of a new

---

[10] Chesterton, The Man Who Was Thursday. Chapter 1.

[11] Ibid.

land, but even into the landscape of a new planet. This was mainly due to the insane yet solid decision of that evening [to join the Anarchists], though partly also to an entire change in the weather and the sky since he entered the little tavern some two hours before. Every trace of the passionate plumage of the cloudy sunset had been swept away, and a naked moon stood in a naked sky. The moon was so strong and full, that (by a paradox often to be noticed) it seemed like a weaker sun. It gave, not the sense of bright moonshine, but rather of a dead daylight.

Over the whole landscape lay a luminous and unnatural discoloration, as of that disastrous twilight which Milton spoke of as shed by the sun in eclipse; so that Syme fell easily into his first thought, that he was actually on some other and emptier planet, which circled round some sadder star.[12]

This is the lunatic nightmare of the Copernican world, where, both by day and by night, Earth spins dizzyingly round the Sun, the whole scene whizzing round like a zoetrope at the rate of nineteen miles a second. This is the world of wild doubt and despair

---

[12] Chesterton, *The Man Who Was Thursday*, Chapter 4.

described by the pessimists whom Chesterton referred to on the eve of his death.

And if we look a little more closely at the opening sentence of the novel we find that alongside the repeated references to the sun is another indication that this is going to be a novel about the difficulties inherent in the Copernican worldview. Interestingly, the word "suburb" appears in that sentence: "The suburb of Saffron Park lay on the sunset side of London . . ." And this should remind us again of Chesterton's 'Defence of Planets' where he says, "We are convinced intellectually that we inhabit a small provincial planet, but we do not feel in the least suburban." Gabriel Syme is literally suburban, he comes from Saffron Park (an invented name, not a real place, as far as I can determine[13]). And when he meets his co-conspirators, he finds that they too are deeply suburban: "Each figure seemed to be, somehow, on the borderland of things; just as their theory was on the borderland of thought."[14] These are displaced and eccentric persons, feeling themselves to be on the periphery of reality, the circumference of truth. But later in the

---

[13] My A-Z map of London lists, under 'Saffron', an Avenue, a Close, a Court, a Hill, a Road, and a Street, but no Park.

[14] Chesterton, *The Man Who Was Thursday*, Chapter 4.

novel this perception is suddenly if temporarily reversed:

> Syme had for a flash the sensation that the cosmos had turned exactly upside down, that all the trees were growing downwards and that all stars were under his feet. Then came slowly the opposite conviction. For the last twenty-four hours the cosmos had really been upside down, but now the capsized universe had come right side up again.[15]

Syme, like the reader, doesn't know whether he is on his head or his heels. He is like the sceptic whom Chesterton describes in the closing pages of *Orthodoxy*, who is "topsy-turvy," "born upside down": "To the modern man the heavens are actually below the earth."[16] The Copernican universe tells him that he is hanging off the planet by his bootsoles, and yet all his natural senses indicate that the Sun is above, not beneath, him. Which is the correct vision? Are the criminals chasing the police or the police chasing the criminals? Are we in a preposterous vehicle in which

---

[15] Chesterton, *The Man Who Was Thursday*, Chapter 8.

[16] G. K. Chesterton, *Orthodoxy*, Project Gutenberg, accessed November 27, 2019, https://www.gutenberg.org/files/16769/16769-h/16769-h.htm.

the passenger is spurring on the horse or does the cabman have the whiphand? Has an old gentleman in grey clothes run away with an elephant or has the elephant eloped with the elderly gent? Is the hornbill a huge yellow beak with a small bird tied on behind it, or vice versa? This oscillating vision – now one thing, now quite the opposite – comes from trying to think in a manner which is cosmologically correct, but perspectivally inhuman. The scientific data tell us that the Sun is fixed and circumnavigable: our senses tell us that it rises in the east, arcs across the sky, and sets in the west.

The Copernican vision of the cosmos, for all its scientific demonstrability, flies in the face of commonsensical, everyday perception. It makes the tail wag the dog, reversing the proper order of things somewhat in the manner described by the prophet Isaiah who asks:

> Shall the axe vaunt itself over him who hews with it,
>
> or the saw magnify itself against him who wields it?
>
> As if a rod should wield him who lifts it,

or as if a staff should lift him who is not wood![17]

The inverted image of reality that Isaiah satirizes here is the same sort of inversion that Chesterton is protesting against in *The Man Who Was Thursday*. The Copernican model runs counter to our experience of reality; none of us really live our daily lives as if Copernicus got it right.

Let us look in more detail at what Chesterton says in his "Defence of Planets":

> In the early days of the world, the discovery of a fact of natural history was immediately followed by the realization of it as a fact of poetry. When man awoke from the long fit of absent-mindedness which is called the automatic animal state, and began to notice the queer facts that the sky was blue and the grass green, he immediately began to use those facts symbolically. Blue, the colour of the sky, became a symbol of celestial holiness; green passed into the language as indicating a freshness verging upon unintelligence. If we had the good fortune to live in a world in which the sky was green and the grass blue, the symbolism would have been different. But for some mysterious reason this habit of realizing

---

[17] Isaiah 10:15.

poetically the facts of science has ceased abruptly with scientific progress, and all the confounding portents preached by Galileo and Newton have fallen on deaf ears. They painted a picture of the universe compared with which the Apocalypse with its falling stars was a mere idyll. They declared that we are all careering through space, clinging to a cannon-ball, and the poets ignore the matter as if it were a remark about the weather. They say that an invisible force holds us in our own armchairs while the earth hurtles like a boomerang; and men still go back to dusty records to prove the mercy of God.[18]

We don't need to go back to the ancient scriptures (those "dusty records") to prove the mercy of God, Chesterton is saying. All we need to do is to become fully awake to God's mercy in not allowing us to spin off this careering cannon-ball we call Planet Earth. Here we are, zipping round the Sun at great speed, yet the centrifugal forces don't fling us off into the furthermost corners of space. God in His mercy has given us the gift of gravity to save us from that fate, and that gift results in Earth

---

[18] G. K. Chesterton, "A Defence of Planets," in The Defendant, Project Gutenberg, accessed November 27, 2019, http://www.gutenberg.org/files/12245/12245-h/12245-h.htm

appearing to be below us and the Heavens above us, not the other way round.

For all that Copernicus may be right scientifically, he is not right poetically or experientially. The Sun really does goes round Earth, *as far as we are concerned,* – a fact that satisfied no less an intellect than that of Sherlock Holmes.[19] It takes a huge effort of imagination to interpret reality otherwise, an effort so huge, so unnatural, so distorting of our normal currents of thought, that it resembles a nightmare.

Chesterton's nightmarish story was, by his own admission, "a very melodramatic kind of moonshine."[20] Moonshine means 'nonsense': only a lunatic believes that the moon shines with its own light. *The Man Who Was Thursday* is a story about an attempt to live nonsensically, as if moonshine were an original and self-sustaining kind of light, rather

---

[19] Dr Watson writes: "I found incidentally that [Holmes] was ignorant of the Copernican Theory and of the composition of the Solar System . . .

"What the deuce is it to me?" he interrupted impatiently; "you say that we go round the sun. If we went round the moon it would not make a pennyworth of difference to me or to my work."

Sir Arthur Conan Doyle, *A Study in Scarlet*, Project Gutenberg, accessed November 27, 2019, https://www.gutenberg.org/files/244/244-h/244-h.htm.

[20] Chesterton, The Man Who Was Thursday, 185.

than a dependent and derivative form of light. The character of Sunday, the President of the Council, Chesterton disclosed, is an "equivocal being;" he wasn't "meant for a serious description of the Deity," but he was mistakenly accorded by certain critics and readers "a temporary respect among those who like the Deity to be so described. But this error was entirely due to the fact that they had read the book but had not read the title-page."[21] The title page is where we are tipped off that this whole story is meant as something approaching a hallucination.

Or perhaps not quite the *whole* story. The tale ends with a beautifully calm and gentle vision at dawn, as Syme sees Rosamond, "the girl with the gold-red hair, cutting lilac before breakfast, with the great unconscious gravity of a girl."[22] These are the very final words of the book and they provide a peaceful resolution of the nightmare. *Unconscious* gravity is evidently being depicted as a good quality, for we know Chesterton to have had supreme respect for the self-forgetfulness of childhood.[23] The

---

[21] Ibid., 185-186.

[22] Chesterton, *The Man Who Was Thursday*, Chapter 15.

[23] Fr. Ronald Knox tells the story of a small child who went to a party at the Chestertons' home. When the boy arrived back, his parents asked whether Mr Chesterton had been very clever. "I don't know about clever," he said, "but you should see him catch buns in his mouf." But this was not mere silliness on Chesterton's part; it was a genuine engagement with the serious business of play as

problem with the post-Copernican cosmos is that, if inhabited with full knowledge and awareness, it makes gravity into something we must consciously, continually, and effortfully recognize. No one can live like that, or not without rendering their world unbearable.

But we might ask: who even tries to live like that? Or, to put it another way, who is the implicit target behind Chesterton's writing of *The Man Who Was Thursday*? Why should he have expended so much imaginative energy depicting a situation which, to all intents and purposes, no one, practically speaking, inhabits?

I suspect Chesterton's implicit target is Nietzsche, whom he tackles in numerous places throughout his writings, – for example, the seventh chapter of *Orthodoxy*, where he calls Nietzsche "a very timid thinker."[24] Nietzsche's ideas were receiving a fair degree of popular exposition in England during the early decades of the twentieth century, thanks in no small part to Chesterton's regular sparring partner, George Bernard Shaw,

---

understood by the visiting children. Knox comments that Chesterton did not "exploit the simplicity of childhood for his own amusement. He entered, with tremendous gravity, into the tremendous gravity of the child." D.J. Conlon (ed.), *G.K. Chesterton: A Half Century of Views* (Oxford: Oxford University Press, 1987), 48.

[24] Chesterton. *Orthodoxy*.

author of the Nietzschean play, *Man and Superman*. Nietzsche believed that Christians worshipped a God who was the source of all heaviness and oppression. God was "the spirit of gravity – through him all things fall."[25] Nietzsche is here using the German word for "gravity" (*die Schwere*) as a kind of theological or metaphysical pun: it conveys two things once (as does the equivalent English word, of course), both the Newtonian force that pulls objects earthwards and a moral force of sombre seriousness. These two effects, both the physical and the moral, derive from the Christian God who is fundamentally an oppressor. God prevents mankind from rising into freedom, and when God dies so does the oppressive "gravity" of His moral law. In *The Gay Science* Nietzsche explains his preference for an alternative kind of grounding, a Dionysian acceptance of good and evil equally, that would somehow keep humanity anchored on earth while yet liberated from the shackling, inhibiting pressure of God's moral demands.[26]

---

[25] Friedrich Nietzsche, *Thus Spake Zarathustra*, Project Gutenberg, accessed November 27, 2019, https://www.gutenberg.org/files/1998/1998-h/1998-h.htm.

[26] I gratefully acknowledge my indebtedness to Mr. Jahdiel Perez, my doctoral student, for the ideas about Nietzsche and gravity expressed in this paragraph.

Nietzsche, however, was trapped by the terms of his own pun, the victim of his own metaphor. Yes, 'gravity' has a literal, physical meaning: the Newtonian pull downwards. But to describe the metaphorical meaning of 'gravity' as an *oppressive* spiritual power is to beg the question. The spiritual power that floors us when we trangress the moral law does so for our own good; that we are being thrust down is evidence of divine justice and mercy, not of divine oppression. As Chesterton writes in *Orthodoxy*, "Satan fell by the force of gravity," but that was not the fault of the moral law, it was the fault of Satan's pride.[27] "Pride cannot rise to levity or levitation. Pride is the downward drag of all things . . . into a sort of selfish seriousness; but one has to rise to a gay self-forgetfulness."[28] The ability to rise is proof of one's humility, of one's self-effacement. "Angels can fly because they can take themselves lightly."[29] But if there were no moral law, the angels would not be flying like birds, they would be merely floating like feathers. Angels – and human beings – are moral agents, responsible for whether they rise or fall. And when they rise, they do not abolish or

---

[27] Chesterton, *Orthodoxy,* Chapter 7.

[28] Ibid.

[29] Ibid.

escape gravity (morality), they transcend it. Rosamond, at the end of *The Man Who Was Thursday*, is beautiful in her "unconscious gravity". She is not thinking of herself, nor of the moral law, but of that for which both she and the moral law have been created: innocent gardening in the cool of the day.

Conclusion

We have seen that Chesterton considers it sheer lunacy – moonshine – to try and live consciously and deliberately within the Copernican view of things, because the Copernican view of things runs counter to our perceptions. And our perceptions matter. We shouldn't be ashamed that we experience reality geocentrically rather than heliocentrically. We can freely admit that we don't see things as they are, we see things as they are *for us*. Only God sees things as they are, and we must not try to usurp His position, must not be "high-minded," for that is what the Fall consists in, becoming dissatisfied with our creaturely and dependent status.[30] To attempt to see things as they are would mean, at the limit, seeing God as He is. But that would be to look directly into the Sun, which hurts and blinds. Only the Son can bear to behold the Father's face.

---

[30] Psalm 131:1-3

[Syme] had turned his eyes so as to see suddenly the great face of Sunday, which wore a strange smile.

"Have you," he cried in a dreadful voice, "have you ever suffered?"

As he gazed, the great face grew to an awful size, grew larger than the colossal mask of Memnon, which had made him scream as a child. It grew larger and larger, filling the whole sky; then everything went black. Only in the blackness before it entirely destroyed his brain he seemed to hear a distant voice saying a commonplace text that he had heard somewhere, "Can ye drink of the cup that I drink of?"[31]

To try to make ourselves divine results in blindness, darkness, madness, as Nietzsche discovered. T.S. Eliot was wiser; he observed in 'Burnt Norton' that "humankind cannot bear very much reality." In this he was merely echoing what Moses was told by God Himself: "No one can see My face and live."[32]

---

[31] Chesterton, *The Man Who Was Thursday*, Chapter 15.

[32] Exodus 33:20.

THE WHITE LIGHT OF WONDER: G.K. CHESTERTON'S PHILOSOPHY OF ART

Melissa Cain Travis

G.K. Chesterton wrote extensively on the subjects of creativity, imagination, and art, and did so as an accomplished artist in his own right. During his distinguished career, he produced an impressive body of poetry, sketches, novels, short stories, essays, and even a few works of drama, many of which clearly reflect his philosophy of art. Any formulation of a philosophy of art from the perspective of Christian humanism is incomplete if it fails to incorporate some of Chesterton's keen insights; he recognized that man, unlike the brute, beholds the world he inhabits with wonder and celebrates that wonder through artistic creation. Chesterton's integrative approach is illuminating and metaphysically satisfying; it is a robust, common-sense philosophy of art that highlights the deficiencies of the materialist alternatives.

Meaning, Imagination, and Play

Chesterton had strong convictions about what it means for man to employ his God-given creative capacity for genuine artistic expression. In "On the True Artist," he argues that "the artist is a person who communicates something . . . it is a question of communication and not merely of what some people call expression. Or rather, strictly speaking, unless it is communication it is not expression."[1] Further on he says: "The artist does ultimately exhibit himself as being intelligent by being intelligible."[2] This doesn't necessarily mean being easy to understand, but definitely being understood. When Chesterton explains that "it is when the work has passed from mind to mind that it becomes a work of art," one is reminded of Leo Tolstoy's words: "The effect of the true work of art is to abolish in the consciousness of the perceiver the distinction between himself and the artist."[3]

---

[1] G.K. Chesterton, "On the True Artist," *Illustrated London News* (November 27, 1926).

[2] Ibid.

[3] G.K. Chesterton, "On the True Artist."; Leo Tolstoy, *What is Art?* (London: Penguin Books, 1995), 121.

That the artist's work needs to be comprehensible and communicate content to the receiver seems right; just as the Creator communicates truths through his creation, so the imagination of the artist calls forth the deep meaning of the world in his acts of re-creation. There is something deeply personal in nature that subtly calls out, and the "ache of the artist" is the desperation to wrest this higher meaning out of obscurity through the imaginative pursuit of objective beauty. Chesterton cautions us that "imaginative does not mean imaginary"; the true artist senses that he "is touching transcendental truths; that his images are shadows of things seen through the veil."[4] Imagination is the power by which these truths are brought into better focus for the sake of understanding. "Imagination is a thing of clear images," he explains, "and the more a thing becomes vague the less imaginative it is."[5] The divine purpose of human art is to reveal and magnify truth about God, man, and the world.

Chesterton believed that wonder, joy, and mirth are characteristic of the divine image in mankind

---

[4] G.K. Chesterton, *The Everlasting Man* (Seaside, Oregon: Watchmaker Publishing, 2013), 65.

[5] G.K. Chesterton, "The Suicide of Thought," *The Illustrated London News* (March 24, 1906).

and inseparable from the imagination. He observed that these things are manifested most clearly in children, who retain a sense of adventure and excitement even toward the mundane; for them, "A tree is something top-heavy and fantastic, a donkey is as exciting as a dragon."[6] The world of childhood is filled with wide-eyed delight about things that most adults, laments Chesterton, regard as prosaic. In his essay, "On Running After One's Hat," he illustrates this with his own characteristically imaginative flair:

> Did you ever hear a small boy complain of having to hang about a railway station and wait for a train? No; for to him to be inside a railway station is to be inside a cavern of wonder and a palace of poetical pleasures. Because to him the red light and the green light on the signal are like a new sun and a new moon. Because to him when the wooden arm of the signal falls down suddenly, it is as if a great king had thrown down his staff as a signal and started a shrieking tournament of trains. I

---

[6] G.K. Chesterton, "The Library of the Nursery," *Lunacy and Letters* (New York: Sheed & Ward, 1958), 27.

myself am of little boys' habit in this matter.[7]

The theme of child-like wonder at the actual world pervades Chesterton's writings on imagination and esthetics. In his autobiography, he recalls the quality of bright lucidity that permeated his childhood: "Mine is a memory of a sort of white light on everything, cutting things out very clearly, and rather emphasizing their solidity...the white light had a sort of wonder in it, as if the world were as new as myself."[8] This white light of wonder best characterizes Chesterton's idea of the genuine aesthetic experience; his use of light as the image for transcendent goodness and truth and his use of darkness and shadow as images for obscurity can be found in many of his writings, regardless of genre. From Chesterton's theistic perspective, the white light of wonder is a glimpse of the eternal and the divine.

It is interesting to note that some materialist philosophers of art recognize this transcendental experience and yet cannot sufficiently explain it. John Dewey, in *Art as Experience*, quotes Ralph

---

[7] G.K. Chesterton, "On Running After One's Hat" in *All Things Considered*, accessed October 7, 2015, http://www.gutenberg.org/files/11505/11505-h/11505-h.htm.

[8] G.K. Chesterton, Autobiography in Everyman Chesterton, 37.

Waldo Emerson's description of such a moment: "Crossing a bare common, in snow puddles, at twilight, under a clouded sky, without having in my thought any occurrence of a special good fortune, I have enjoyed a perfect exhilaration. I am glad to the brink of fear."[9] In response to the passage, Dewey admits that he cannot "see any way of accounting for the multiplicity of experiences of this kind (something of the same quality being found in every spontaneous and uncoerced esthetic response)."[10] He describes it as a "mystic aspect of acute esthetic surrender, that renders it so akin as an experience to what religionists term ecstatic communion," yet he explains it away as "dispositions acquired in primitive relationships of the living being to its surroundings."[11] He maintains that sensuous experience has an infinite capacity "to absorb into itself meanings and values that in and of themselves...would be designated 'ideal' and 'spiritual.'"[12] However, on Dewey's materialist view, nothing can have inherent meaning in this objective

---

[9] Ralph Waldo Emerson, *Works of Ralph Waldo Emerson* (Boston: Houghton, Osgood, and Co, 1880), 5:17.

[10] John Dewey, *Art as Experience* (New York: Berkeley Publishing Group, 2005), 29.

[11] Ibid., 29.

[12] Dewey, Art as Experience. 29.

sense; there is only quasi-meaning that humans ascribe to the sensuous world. By contrast, in Chesterton's theistic perspective, real meaning saturates the cosmos and shines through the material creation as well as the imaginative creations of man.

Chesterton urges us to see that the imaginative state of mind is one in which the ordinary, even the inconvenient, is an opportunity for wonder and delight. He opens and concludes "On Running After One's Hat" by wistfully envisioning the flooding of his hometown that has occurred while he is away on holiday, an event the other residents likely find irritatingly inconvenient. "Now that it has the additional splendour of great sheets of water," he muses, "there must be something quite incomparable in the landscape (or waterscape) of my own romantic town. Battersea must be a vision of Venice."[13] He imagines the green-grocer and butcher gliding swiftly and gracefully through the shimmering, watery streets-turned-canals, using gondolas to deliver their goods. "I do not think that it is altogether fanciful or incredible to suppose that even the floods in London may be accepted and

_____

[13] Chesterton, "On Running After One's Hat."

enjoyed poetically," he muses.[14] Perhaps the flood waters are an inconvenience, but an inconvenience "is only one aspect, and that the most unimaginative and accidental aspect of a really romantic situation" and "an adventure is only an inconvenience rightly considered."[15]

Chesterton emphasized the wonder-inducing qualities of whimsy and nonsense for communicating truths about reality, including (and perhaps especially) theological truths. Thomas Peters explains that, for Chesterton, "it is in the God-given realms of joy and play and frivolity and nonsense that the imagination tends to find its most fruitful harvest."[16] In his essay, "A Defence of Nonsense," Chesterton writes that the foundational idea behind nonsense is the idea of escape, "of escape into a world where things are not fixed horribly in an eternal appropriateness."[17] The wonder of creation needs to be recovered, but

---

[14] Chesterton, "On Running After One's Hat."

[15] Ibid.

[16] Thomas Peters, *The Christian Imagination* (San Francisco: Ignatius Press, 2000), 126.

[17] G.K. Chesterton, "A Defence of Nonsense" in *The Defendant*, accessed October 7, 2015, http://www.gutenberg.org/files/12245/12245-h/12245-h.htm#A_DEFENCE_OF_NONSENSE

a thing cannot be completely wonderful so long as it remains sensible. So long as we regard a tree as an obvious thing, naturally and reasonably created for a giraffe to eat, we cannot properly wonder at it. It is when we consider it as a prodigious wave of the living soil sprawling up to the skies for no reason in particular that we take off our hats...This is the side of things which tends most truly to spiritual wonder.[18]

Not only is God the creator of the sensible world and his image-bearing human beings, he is also the creator of laughter, play, and our imaginative capacity.[19] The artist, through his painting, sketches, poetry, drama, prose, or sculpture, should utilize nonsense in a manner that ignites a fresh sense of wonder about things, an escape from the sterile, scientistic half-truths of the world. Says Chesterton: "It might reasonably be maintained that the true object of all human life is play. Earth is a task garden; Heaven is a playground...to be so good that one can treat everything as a joke—that may be,

---

[18] Chesterton, "A Defense of Nonsense."

[19] Peters, The Christian Imagination. 127.

perhaps the real end and final holiday of human souls."[20]

On Poetry

A fine example of Chesterton's philosophy in practice is *Greybeards at Play*, a short collection of fanciful poetry embellished with drawings that may well be described as Seussian. He illustrates his poem entitled "The Oneness of the Philosopher with Nature" with a black-and-white sketch of an aged, bespectacled scholar reclining upon the sphere of the earth, gazing into the heavens, with a smiling star perched on the end of his nose (figure 1). The poem begins, "I love to see the little stars / All dancing to one tune; / I think quite highly of the Sun, / And kindly of the Moon."[21] The disproportionately large philosopher and the allusion to the aesthetic appeal and cyclical regularity of the starry skies reminds one how wondrous a thing it is that rational man, unlike all other creatures of the world, can gaze into the heavens and contemplate the orderly nature of the cosmos. Using simple rhyming verse

---

[20] G.K. Chesterton, "Oxford From Without" in *All Things Considered,* accessed November 10, 2015, http://www.gutenberg.org/files/11505/11505-h/11505-h.htm.

[21] G.K. Chesterton, *Greybeards at Play* in *The Collected Works of G.K. Chesterton Vol. X* (San Francisco: Ignatius Press, 2000), 355.

and the nonsensical, cartoonish image, Chesterton conveys profound truth in a lighthearted, memorable way. Man may not be a physical giant relative to the size of the universe or even the earth, but he stands far above the rest of creation in spirit, intellect, and significance.

Art for fun's sake was another hallmark of Chesterton's philosophy, and one that is evident even in his early art. It was during his school years that he met Edmund Clerihew Bentley, who invented the four-line, pseudo-biographical poetry that came to be known as the "clerihew."[22] Typically, the clerihew was used to poke good-natured fun at a public personality, though biographical content was not a hard-and-fast rule. During their school days, Bentley wrote many of these comical quatrains, and Chesterton illustrated them in addition to writing clerihews of his own.[23] A particularly amusing illustration (Figure 2) is the one Chesterton drew for the following Bentley clerihew:

> The Art of Biography
> Is different from Geography.
> Geography is about Maps,

---

[22] Peters, The Christian Imagination. 137.

[23] Ibid.

But Biography is about Chaps.[24]

The stylistic similarity between this early drawing and the much later one for "The Oneness of the Philosopher with Nature" (Figure 1) is striking; Chesterton's frivolity is a shining thread that runs throughout all the decades of his work.

Chesterton's own clerihews can be found in scholarly collections of his poetry. He co-authored many with Bentley, but some were exclusively his own, including this piece:

> The Spanish think Cervantes
> Equal to half a dozen Dantes;
> An opinion resented most bitterly
> By the people of Italy.[25]

The clerihew was, more than anything, a pleasurable pastime, an act of playful creativity meant to lighten the heart of both artist and reader. Moreover, it should not be forgotten that for Chesterton, play draws one closer to heaven.

While Chesterton highly valued the elements of nonsense and frivolity as means of expression, he had a sober side, particularly when it

---

[24] E.C. Bentley, *The Complete Clerihews* (Cornwall: Stratus Books Ltd., 2008), 1.

[25] Chesterton, *Collected Works Vol. X*, 344.

came to his formal poetry. He did not endorse the idea of completely unrestricted art; he believed that form had much to do with the purpose of an artwork. In his polemic essay, "The Slavery of Free Verse," he condemns the trend away from structured rhythm and rhyme in modern poetry. Despite the use of the term "free" to describe the style, the perceived emancipation of poetry is actually an enslavement, he argues.[26] It does not liberate the soul as truly poetical language does; it does not incite wonder. Chesterton fancies that "if a man were really free, he would talk in rhythm and even in rhyme."[27] Poetry, he says, is much more representative of reality than crude, disjointed language, because "at the back of everything, existence begins with a harmony and not a chaos; and, therefore, when we really spread our wings and find a wider freedom, we find it in something more continuous and recurrent...[28] He gives the rather humorous example of requesting food in poetical language, and suggests that asking for a potato

---

26 G.K. Chesterton, "The Slavery of Free Verse" in *In Defense of Sanity* (San Francisco: Ignatius Press, 2000), 155.

27 Ibid.. 155-156.

28 Ibid., 156.

using a poem would be both a more romantic and more *realistic* image of the potato:

> For a potato is a poem; it is even an ascending scale of poems; beginning at the root, in subterranean grotesques in the gothic manner, with humps like the deformities of a goblin and eyes like a beast of Revelation, and rising up through the green shades of the earth to a crown that has the shape of stars and the hue of heaven.[29]

This is another example of Chesterton's belief that the imagination, when applied to the seemingly prosaic or even the ugly, inspires fresh wonder.

The creation of man is a theme that frequently appears in Chesterton's poetry, further attesting to the importance he placed upon one's conception of human nature. In "The Germ," the creation of Adam from the dust of the earth is told through a series of statements made to Adam by God, each prefaced with "God spake to the red Adam."[30] The poem beautifully communicates the place of mankind in the created order and God's sovereignty over the course of the world:

---

[29] Chesterton, *In Defense of Sanity*, 156.

[30] Chesterton, *Collected Works Vol. X*, 65-66.

God spake to the red Adam:
"For all thy works hath a breath sufficed;
Live: defy me, Prometheus: serve me,
Christ"

God spake to the red Adam:
"Curse my universe, curse thy brood.
I made thee for an end and find thee
Good."[31]

Note also the allusion to the incarnation as the key to God's relationship to man. Chesterton's Christian theology shines through his structured verse in a provocative and imaginative way. In "The Missing Link," which Chesterton penned around 1898, the theme of man as a revolution, not a mere evolution, is apparent:

The Brute, four legged with a hanging head
Plodded the ground in an age long dead,
Earth was the only sky he knew;
Stars were blood-red and gold and blue
Till some hour, whose tale is given
Faint in the secret scrolls of heaven,
Some great portent filled the sky.
And leaping at light, the brute sprang high
Pawing at heaven: and fell not again,

---

[31] Chesterton, *Collected Works*, 66.

And man stood crowned in brow and

brain.[32]

The poetic language and form used here inspires contemplative wonder regarding the grand cosmic shift that occurred when a certain creature became fully human, having rationality and spiritual awareness bestowed as the image of God. The very title of the poem implies that science does not, indeed cannot, answer the metaphysical questions surrounding the unprecedented, unparalleled phenomenon that is mankind.

On Fairy Tales

Recall Chesterton's conviction that, when seen in the "white light of wonder," the mundane becomes extraordinary. "The function of the imagination," he says, "is not to make strange things settled, so much as to make settled things strange; not so much to make wonders facts as to make facts wonders."[33] Perhaps a succinct statement about his philosophy of art would be that true art helps the observer recover a sense of astonishment at the

---

[32] Chesterton, *Collected Works,* 258.

[33] G.K. Chesterton, "A Defence of China Shepherdesses" in *The Defendant,* accessed November 10, 2015, http://www.online-literature.com/chesterton/the-defendant/7/.

world as it really is — infused with deep meaning. In the introduction he wrote for the biography *George MacDonald and His Wife*, Chesterton named MacDonald's *The Princess and the Goblin* as the one story that had influenced him more than any other; he described it as "a book that has made a difference to my whole existence, which helped me to see things in a certain way from the start ... it remains the most real, the most realistic, in the exact sense of the phrase the most like life."[34] He says, "When I read it as a child, I felt that the whole thing was happening inside a real human house, not essentially unlike the house I was living in, which also had staircases and rooms and cellars. This is where the fairy-tale differed from many other fairy-tales; above all, this is where the philosophy differed from many other philosophies."[35] MacDonald's fairy tale achieved the feat of "making all the ordinary staircases and doors and windows into magical things."[36]

---

[34] G.K. Chesterton, Introduction to *George MacDonald and His Wife* (by Greville M. MacDonald. 1924), accessed October 23, 2015, http://www.pford.stjohnsem.edu/ford/cslewis/documents/macdonald/GKC%20on%20GM.pdf.

[35] Ibid.

[36] Ibid.

The Princess and the Goblin is a story about a young princess living in a mountain castle that is plagued by demons who invade it through the cellars. The castle stairways are the princess's escape from the evil; she climbs up to higher rooms, but mysteriously, the stairs sometimes take her to a new room she has never seen before, where a great-grandmother — a fairy-godmother figure — speaks comforting words of encouragement. "There is," says Chesterton, "something not only imaginative but intimately true about the idea of the goblins being below the house and capable of besieging it from the cellars. When the evil things besieging us do appear, they do not appear outside but inside."[37] Chesterton recognized MacDonald's genius as the ability to place the fairy tale "inside of the ordinary story and not the outside":

> The commonplace allegory takes what it regards as the commonplaces or conventions necessary to ordinary men and women, and tries to make them pleasant or picturesque by dressing them up as princesses or goblins or good fairies. But George MacDonald did really believe that people were princesses and goblins

---

[37] Chesterton, *George MacDonald.*

and good fairies, and he dressed them up
as ordinary men and women.[38]

It seems that MacDonald sensed that preternatural light of clarity bathing the ordinary, that he saw "the same sort of halo round every flower and bird."[39] But, insists Chesterton, this is not the same thing as mere *appreciation* of the beauty of flowers and birds: "A heathen can feel that and remain heathen, or in other words remain sad. It is a certain special sense of significance, which the tradition that most values it calls sacramental."[40] A psychological response to an aesthetically appealing object is one thing, but authentic wonder at the beauty in the world is an experience of the transcendent.

In one of his better-known fairy stories, *The Coloured Lands*, Chesterton beautifully communicates his philosophy and emulates what he so admired about *The Princess and the Goblin*. The tale involves a ten-year-old boy, Tommy, who is sitting, hot, bored, and dejected, in the grass by the country cottage his family has taken for the summer:

---

[38] Chesterton, *George MacDonald*.

[39] Ibid.

[40] Ibid.

The cottage had a bare white-washed all; and at that moment it seemed to Tommy very bare. The summer sky was of a blank blue, which at that moment seemed to him very blank. The dull yellow thatch looked very dull and rather dusty; and the row of flower-pots in front of him, with red flowers in them, looked irritatingly straight, so that he wanted to knock some of them down like ninepins. Even the grass around him moved him only to pluck it up in a vicious way; almost as if he were wicked enough to wish it was his sister's hair.[41]

Suddenly, Tommy is aware of a young man, having appeared from out of nowhere and walking towards him. The man wears a pale grey suit and has long, pale hair, both of which glow whitish in the summer sunlight, and his appearance is made even stranger by his blue-lensed spectacles, a floppy straw hat, and the peacock green Japanese parasol he carries. The reader is struck with the impression of something fantastical just barely cloaked in plausibility. This new character offers Tommy the opportunity to peer through the blue spectacles to see what a blue world would look like. Then, the man produces pairs of red, yellow, and green spectacles

---

[41] G.K. Chesterton, *The Coloured Lands* (Mineola, NY: Dover Publications, 2009), 17.

for Tommy to try on in succession, and the boy is startled by each new colored-land experience.

The man reveals that when he himself was a boy, he "also used to sit on the grass and wonder what to do with myself . . . I also thought that everything might look different if the colours were different; if I could wander about on blue roads between blue fields and go on wandering till all was blue."[42] He recounts meeting a powerful wizard who granted his wish, and tells of his monochromatic excursions into actual lands of blue, green, yellow, and red. "What did you find out?" Tommy asks, and the man replies:

> Well, do you know, it is a curious fact that in a rose-red city you cannot really see any roses. Everything is a great deal too red. Your eyes are tired until it might just as well all be brown. After I had been walking for ten minutes on scarlet grass under a scarlet sky and scarlet trees, I called out in a loud voice, "Oh, this is all a mistake."[43]

The wizard had then transported him to a mystical place with mountainous, multi-colored, layered topography, "the great original place from which all the colours came, like the paint-box of

---

[42] Chesterton, *The Coloured Lands*, 21.

[43] Ibid., 24.

creation."[44] Impatient, the wizard instructed him to paint the world he really wanted upon a great transparent wall of watery light situated in a great chasm between the hills. The young man says that, after painting for a while, "I slowly discovered what I was doing; which is what very few people ever discover in this world. I found I had put back, bit by bit, the whole of that picture over there in front of us."[45] The newly painted world turned out to be the summer cottage with the thatched roof, white walls, and red flowers in a straight row, all situated under a brilliant blue summer sky. "That is how they come to be there," explains the young man, and Tommy sits staring at the cottage in wide-eyed wonder, as if truly seeing it for the very first time.[46]

The moral of the tale is that the reality of the world is the most astounding thing of all; one only needs their vision freshly baptized in order to wonder anew at the splendor and, more fundamentally, the very *existence* of the world. This is the idea upon which Chesterton's philosophy is founded. The failure to understand it is, as Chesterton might have phrased it, what's wrong with the world of modern art. The modern artists, he

---

[44] Chesterton, *The Coloured Lands*, 27.

[45] Ibid., 28.

[46] Ibid.

says, "are now trying to do bad work in order to have something to wonder at" and are devoted to "the experiment of making ugly things, that they might recover an astonishment no longer accorded to beautiful things."[47] The pitiable modern artist torments himself, "pinching himself to see if he is awake, not having about him the real white daylight of wonder to keep him wide-awake."[48] But this is the wrong road, a wild goose chase, Chesterton warns; people do not need more artists capable of producing shocking works, they need to be restored in their ability to wonder at common things.

A Chestertonian Aesthetic

Chesterton's articulation of his philosophy of art employs none of the technical jargon typical in aesthetic theory but a great deal of common sense. The way human beings actually experience the world around them, including their aesthetic perception and artistic propensities, is a peculiarity of our species that is explained well by Christian theism. Man reflects the Creator, in whose image he is made, by creating works such as poetry and imaginative prose that celebrate the world. Works of

---

[47] Chesterton, "Are the Artists Going Mad?" 277.

[48] Ibid., 278.

art should evoke a sense of wonder at reality, a kind of wonder that is arguably more common among children, but that Chesterton believed can and should be recovered in adults. Wonder is the very essence of authentic aesthetic sensibility, and the proper goal of art. Given theism, wonder is more than merely a subjective mental experience; its ultimate object is the transcendent. True art propels the mind upward through its wonder-inciting illumination of sensible reality. Chesterton's view that man is more than matter in motion elevates art to its proper place and gives it authentic significance. He believed that in imaginative expression — which often includes whimsy, nonsense, and drawing out the poetical in the seemingly mundane —man's awareness of transcendental goodness and truth can grow and flourish. Contrary to materialism, the human aesthetic experience attests to inherent meaning, a higher reality, and the uniqueness of mankind among all other creatures. Man perceives real meaning in the world around him, and he expresses this meaning through his artistry, communicating truth to his fellow man by reawakening the innate sense of wonder at *what is*.

Figure 1

Figure 2

THE HAPPY HOME TO WHICH WE ARE ALL FARING

Rebekah Valerius

Henrik Ibsen's brilliant "A Doll's House" has arguably been one of the most influential plays in modern times. Though scandalous at the time of its production in 1879, the story depicting the dramatic undoing of a Scandinavian family quickly became a symbol for the feminist movement in the Western world. Born just five years earlier, G.K. Chesterton grew up in a world buzzing with debate over the play and its negative depiction of domesticity as narrow and confining. It should come as no surprise that references to Ibsen and his doll's house appeared in many of Chesterton's writings. In recent years, the buzz shows no sign of subsiding with "A Doll's House" being the most performed play in 2006, the centennial of Ibsen's death.[1] Below is an imagined encounter between its heroine, Nora, and Chesterton. The scene is a railway station in Norway, early in the morning, several days after Nora has left her husband and children.

His words rang in my ears as I stood alone on the train platform.

> *. . . But no man would sacrifice his honour for the one he loves.[2]*

A vast blanket of clouds stretched across the sky with a tent of impenetrable gray. Somewhere in the distance a clock tower sounded, the only evidence of dawn beneath the grim canopy. It was as if the sun lacked the strength to rise and run its course this bleak, mid-winter morning; the world would be deprived of its warmth today. Only a few specks of snow dared to enliven the dull surroundings.

I welcomed the cold and sullen setting; it was an appropriate companion to my heart's icy resolve. My train wasn't set to arrive for at least an hour but I remained outside, deliberately avoiding the warmth

---

[1] It has now been translated into over seventy-eight languages and made into countless film adaptations (One starring a young Sir Anthony Hopkins can be found at https://youtu.be/qnX8XSKs18c).

[2] Henrik Ibsen, *A Doll's House* (Seattle: Amazon Classics), 84.

of the inner station's hearth. This was my own sunless dawn.

As the chill penetrated my thin cloak and shawl, I thought of how these past eight years I had 'bought the simplest and cheapest things' for myself so that I could pay off the debt to Krogstad – the debt I incurred to save my dying husband.[3] These were my sole possessions now, along with the small bag I clutched as if my life depended upon it.

I spoke aloud to the lonely scene before me, "Awake, O sleeper, and arise from your dream! No more husband. No more children. That doll's house must be left behind; that door shut forever. Only then will I find myself."

"Find myself," a man's voice from behind me repeated quietly, almost to himself, "Yet, 'one may understand the cosmos, but never the ego; the self is more distant than any star. Thou shalt love the Lord thy God; but thou shalt not know thyself.'"[4]

Startled, I turned to see a bulk of fur as big as a bear sitting on the bench behind me.

---

[3] Ibsen, A Doll's House, 17.

[4] G.K. Chesterton, *Orthodoxy* (New York: Open Roads Media, 2018), 58.

"'Ah, but he that will lose his life, the same shall save it,'" the cloaked figure continued.[5]

"Lose my life?" I asked, turning to him completely, "I've not had a life to lose. I have to find it first."

"No life to lose?" the giant questioned, looking at me with a pair of piercing blue eyes, "You certainly seem alive to me, yet perhaps not for long on this frozen platform. Though a desolate train station in the dead of winter is surely an inconvenience just waiting to become an adventure, one can't enjoy an adventure if they've been turned to ice! Come, let us wait inside and let me introduce myself. Mr. G.K. Chesterton at your service, and you must be Mrs. Helmer. I was hoping to meet you here."

"I prefer to remain outside and I am no longer Mrs. Helmer. My name is Nora," I replied coldly. "Mr. Chesterton, have we met?"

"Well, I have met you – or, at least, I am well acquainted with your story. You haven't met me, but that is why I am here. I'm hoping to be of some help to you and to the many that will follow you."

"Follow me?"

---

[5] Chesterton, *Orthodoxy*, 109.

"Yes, *the hundreds of thousands of women who have sacrificed their honour for the ones they love.*"[6]

But those were my words! That is what I told Torvald when the awful truth came crashing in that *the most wonderful thing of all* would not happen this Christmastide.[7] My husband would not risk everything for me, as I had done for him. Our marriage was nothing to him when compared to his precious reputation.

"Did Torvald send you? You can tell him that I remain as resolved as ever to leave."

"I am sorry," Mr. Chesterton remarked, "This will be confusing, but your husband did not send me. I have never met him, though I know him as well as I know you. Years from now, a brilliant dramatist will transform these past few days of your life into a powerful play, and it will become a symbol of everything that is wrong with hearth and home. The culture will have a similar reaction as yours, too, and that is what I am here to prevent if I can."

"Sir, I am not at all sure of what you are saying – it's all so strange – but if true, then I am glad many will follow me," I replied, adding with passion, "Hundreds of thousands of women will be set free

---

[6] Ibsen, A Doll's House. 84.

[7] Ibid., 86.

from the role of domestic doll to distinguish themselves, free from the dominance of men."

Rising from his seat, Mr. Chesterton said gently, "Come now, let us move inside to the warmth. I'll ask the porter to add more logs to the fire." Moving towards the door, he added, "Do you know that 'Nora' means 'honour'?"

There's that word again! Strange how I had not made the connection. Of all things for Torvald to prefer to me *. . . but no man would sacrifice his honour for the one he loves.*[8]

Suddenly, "a great wind sprang high in the west, like a wave of unreasonable happiness, and tore eastward across" the platform, "trailing with it the frosty scent of forests and the cold intoxication of the sea."[9] The snow began to fall in real defiance of the gloom, brightening it with a blaze of white. My heart warmed slightly at the blast of freshness.

Mr. Chesterton began laughing uncontrollably. As I turned to see his laughter's cause, the sight of the huge man struggling to enter the doorway made me laugh, too – something I had not done for days.

Good heavens, he was stuck!

---

[8] Ibsen, A *Doll's House*. 84.

[9] G.K. Chesterton, *Manalive* (Seattle: Amazon Digital Services), 1.

"Mr. Chesterton, you might try entering sideways."

"'I have no sideways!'" he snorted.[10] Eventually, with the aid of the porter inside, we were able to maneuver the side-less man through the door.

Still laughing, he remarked, "Humor can get in under the door while seriousness is still fumbling at the handle."[11]

Even so, I thought to myself with a smile, humor might need to shed a few pounds. Evidence of too many macaroons, perhaps?

Oh, the bitter thought of macaroons! That confection represented everything that was wrong with my marriage: Torvald's incessant patronizing, as if I were but a simple child who needed the guidance of a wise superior. Sadness overtook me as I entered the waiting room. I sank into a seat by the hearth across from Mr. Chesterton as the porter tended to the fire. A spasm of exhaustion spread across my entire body, as if I'd been carrying a full

---

[10] G.K. Chesterton as quoted in "G.K. Chesterton," *Christianity Today,* accessed October 9, 2019.
https://www.christianitytoday.com/history/people/musiciansartis tsandwriters/g-k-chesterton.html,

11 Darin Moore, "A Chestertonian Thanksgiving," *The Imaginative Conservative,* November 22, 2012, accessed October 1, 2019. https://theimaginativeconservative.org/2012/11/a-chestertonian-thanksgiving.html,

washbasin that had frozen over after a long, cold night.

Mr. Chesterton was speaking to himself as he sat down across from me.

"'If we were to-morrow morning snowed up in the street in which we live, we should step suddenly into a much larger and much wilder world than we have ever known.'[12]Yes, 'the man who lives in a small community lives in a much larger world. He knows much more of the fierce varieties and uncompromising divergences of men.'[13] Another paradox!" he clapped his hands with delight, 'as if he had caught sight of some secret in the very shape of the universe hidden from the universe itself.'[14]

His laughter stopped as he turned towards me. "Why are you leaving your family?"

"'The most original modern thinkers,'" I solemnly replied, "the revolutionaries 'say that what we want most is ... to find ourselves in untrodden paths, and to do unprecedented things: to break with the past and belong to the future.'[15] I have decided to

---

[12] G.K. Chesterton, *Heretics*, (New York City: John Lane Co, 1919) 78.

[13] Ibid.

[14] G.K. Chesterton, *The Everlasting Man* (Tacoma, WA: Angelico Press, 2013), 26.

[15] Chesterton, *Manalive*, 93.

take their advice and break with the oppressive convention of marriage, to find a way in the world on my own terms and not on the terms that tradition has dictated."

"Ah, tradition," he said, "I have never been able to understand why we are taught to be suspicious of tradition, as if it was some sort of dictatorial system that was intrinsically 'opposed to democracy. It is obvious that tradition is only democracy extended through time. It is trusting to a consensus of common human voices rather than to some isolated or arbitrary' reaction or mood."[16]

"I wrote a story once where the hero left his home," he continued, "From all appearances, he seemed to be rejecting tradition, too. Do you know what he found? He discovered that 'it is really wicked and dangerous for a man to run away from his wife."[17]

"And why is it dangerous?" I inquired.

"'Why, because nobody can find him,'" he answered, "'and we all want to be found.'[18] Those modern thinkers talk of revolution as if it's merely a breaking out, but they forget that word contains a

---

[16] Chesterton, *Orthodoxy*, 129.

[17] Chesterton, *Manalive*, 93.

[18] Ibid.

very important idea – *revolve*. When something revolves, it eventually returns. 'Every revolution, like a repentance, is a return ... Don't you see that all these real leaps and destructions and escapes are only attempts to get back to Eden— to something we have had, to something we at least have heard of? Don't you see that one only breaks the fence or shoots the moon in order to get home?'"[19,20]

"Mr. Chesterton, at home I was nothing more than a doll playing a game. I do not want to return to that! I was a doll-wife to Torvald, just as I had been a doll-child to my father. I treated my children as doll-children, too. We were playing house just as we had been taught by tradition."[21]

"And now that you have outgrown dolls, they must be discarded so that you can find yourself," he replied with a sadness that stabbed my heart.

"But I am not ready to be a real wife and mother!" I replied in my defense. "I really had no choice in the matter, too. I was just doing what was expected of me."

"Ready? Why, you are already a wife and mother. Choice aside, it's a strange superstition that

---

[19] Chesterton, *Manalive*, 90.

[20] Ibid., 93.

[21] Ibsen, A Doll's House. 80.

believes the act of shutting the door on one's family will break its bonds.[22] It's more superstitious than the tradition of sacramental marriage, in fact. Abandoning your children in their beds does not make them less yours. Yours is a dangerous reaction, too, for its brutal logic will be worked out in future generations. Years from now, children will not only be abandoned in their beds, but in the womb as well – inspired by your vision of self-determination."

"But how can a childish person such as myself, who is so unacquainted with the world, raise children?" I asked. This was precisely what Torvald had concluded, after all.

"By becoming more child-like, actually!" he exclaimed, and at this, his eyes brightened and he leaped from his seat with excitement.[23] He continued, moving about the room with a lightness that was surprising given his vastness.

"What is wrong with regarding your house like a doll's house?' he asked. "'The whole aim of a house is

---

[22] "While free love seems to me a heresy, divorce does really seem to me a superstition. It is not only more of a superstition than free love, but much more of a superstition than strict sacramental marriage; and this point can hardly be made too plain." G.K. Chesterton. *The Superstition of Divorce* (Seattle: Amazon Digital Services, 2010), 6.

[23] See "A Second Childhood" by G.K. Chesterton, from the *The Ballad of Saint Barbara and Other Verses*. https://alongthebeam.com/2019/08/29/a-second-childhood/

to be a doll's house. Don't you remember, when you were a child, how those little windows WERE windows, while the big windows weren't? A child has a doll's house, and shrieks when a front door opens inwards. A banker has a real house, yet how numerous are the bankers who fail to emit the faintest shriek when their real front doors open inwards.'"[24]

I could not imagine Torvald shrieking with child-like delight.

"We only run from our houses because we have grown too dull for them – like the man in my story. In fact, we aren't really running at all. Because the house is so much more alive than us, it runs, and we can't keep up! All have sinned and have grown old and too weak to run,"[25] he said with a twinkle in his eyes.

Try as I may, I could not help but chuckle at the mental picture of the elephantine man chasing a miniature house.

"'The doll's house is that happy home to which we are all faring,'" he laughed along with me, "'if it looks small it is because it is far away.'"[26]

---

[24] Chesterton, *Manalive*, 92.

[25] Chesterton, *Orthodoxy*, 67.

[26] G.K. Chesterton, "What a Home Means: Wildness of Domesticity" *The Guyra Argus*, November 11, 1909, accessed October

His words were very strange, yet oddly pleasing, for he delivered them with such eager delight. This was not at all like Torvald's solemn moralizing that had annoyed me so much. Mr. Chesterton made virtue look positively inviting.

Would Torvald have understood him? Probably not. Though he held to the same traditions, Torvald took himself far too seriously to resonate with Mr. Chesterton's child-like joy. Torvald was quite an honorable man, yes, but he was all honour and no happiness. He cared only for truth, and his truth was as pitiless as one of his banking calculations.[27] He would have regarded Mr. Chesterton as rather unserious, I'm afraid. The thought of this made me angry.

"So I must honour my marriage vows, even though I do not know *what* marriage is or *who* it is that I married?"

"What is marriage?" Mr. Chesterton asked, coming to a sudden standstill and gazing out the

---

1, 2019,
https://trove.nla.gov.au/newspaper/article/174452086/20572707.

[27] "The modern world is full of the old Christian virtues gone mad. The virtues have gone mad because they have been isolated from each other and are wandering alone. Thus some scientists care for truth; and their truth is pitiless. Thus some humanitarians only care for pity; and their pity (I am sorry to say) is often untruthful." G.K. Chesterton, *Orthodoxy*, 28-29.

window as if to some faraway place. "The wisest Man that ever walked the earth was asked this question by the religious leaders of His day. They had lost its meaning, too. His reply indicated that marriage 'is an ideal altogether outside time; difficult at any period; impossible at no period.'"[28]

"You say this man spoke of marriage as something difficult and I can agree, but marriage as an ideal? Are there really such things as ideals? I'm not at all sure anymore," I sighed.

"Difficult marriages to run from and no ideal marriage to run towards ... Ah, this is the real problem with today's revolutions, isn't it?" he continued, his sight remaining fixed on the window and the rapidly falling snow beyond. "Revolutionists can rail against imperfection, but they have no perfection towards which to aim. They have all 'definite images of evil, and ... no definite image of good. To us light must be henceforward the dark thing – the thing of which we cannot speak. To us, as to Milton's devils in Pandemonium, it is darkness that is visible. The human race, according to religion, fell once, and in falling gained knowledge of good and of evil. Now we have fallen a second

---

[28] Chesterton, *The Everlasting Man,* 169.

time, and only the knowledge of evil remains to us.'"[29]

Turning to me, he continued, "With regards to your vows, we live in an age that has kept the conventions but has forgotten the commandments - the ideals - from which they spring. Indeed, like you, it doubts that there are ideals, and this is a perilous predicament. The moment the convention gets hard, as all the best conventions do, we destroy them. But there is no Eden to return to in this age that is haunted by such a negative spirit.[30] It's all darkness and no light. Nothing can fill the gap but the lonely philosophy of finding one's self."

"You see, the truth is that the ideal of marriage is too alive for you and Torvald – it's running from you both. That's why you can't see it, so you doubt its existence. Chase it! Start by *honouring* your vow, *Nora*. That's the path to take to find it."

"There is hope for Torvald, too," he continued gently as he saw my face fall, "Now that he has experienced what the wise, old poets called the 'coldness of Chloe,' which he very well deserved given his ignorance of your dignity as a woman

---

[29] Chesterton, *Heretics*, 10.

[30] Chesterton, *Heretics*. 7.

(another ideal that is especially Christian).[31] I have often observed that 'the way to love anything is to realize that it might be lost.'[32] I believe he fears losing his *Nora*, now, more than his *honour*."

"But Torvald and I are completely incompatible!" I cried, unable to countenance the thought of returning to him.

"I have known many happy marriages," Mr. Chesterton laughed heartily, "but never a compatible one. The whole aim of marriage is to fight through and survive the instant when incompatibility becomes unquestionable. For a man and a woman, as such, are incompatible."[33]

"But what about my duty to myself? My education?" I sulked, perturbed by his laughter.

"Ah, yes, breaking out into the world to find yourself. Tell me, what has the world taught your husband? Torvald might have been instructed in the narrow domains of politics and economics, but he wasn't taught to value the vast universe inside his own home where the most costly transactions occur. He learned to view the domestic cosmos as a

---

[31] G.K. Chesterton, *What's Wrong with the World*, (San Francisco: Ignatius Press, 1994) 57.

[32] G.K. Chesterton, *Tremendous Trifles*, (Jersey City: Start Publishing, 2013), Location 403.

[33] Chesterton, What's Wrong with the World, 24.

plaything - the easier lesson by far. Yet, 'the place where babies are born, where men die, where the drama of mortal life is acted, is not an office or a shop or a bureau. It is something much smaller in size and much larger in scope."[34]

"Yes, Torvald always underestimated the difficulty of running a house," I remarked angrily. "He merely returned home to pet his captive bird – his Sky-Lark as he called me– to play house with her as long as she kept out of his more important business. The outer world was more real for him. We had 'never exchanged so much as one serious word about serious things' from the moment we met."[35]

"Hm. Serious things," he remarked. "Torvald referred to you as his little Sky-Lark not knowing that all his world turned upon such a serious lark. That lark saved his life when the world of work would have him perish.[36] Yours were not the actions of an unknowing doll. They were those of a domestic empress doing her best to protect her family for, unlike the happy doll's house, death lurks at the doors of our lesser abodes."

---

[34] G.K. Chesterton "Women in the Workplace—and at Home" *Illustrated London News.* December 18, 1926.

[35] Ibsen, *A Doll's House*, 79.

[36] It is indicated that Torvald's previous illness was a result of being overworked.

This was too much for me. As tears began to flood my eyes, I fought them off angrily.

"Torvald cares more for his honour than me! When I was willing to die for him! *No man would sacrifice his honour for the one he loves*, he said."

"Terrible, terrible words, yes," he said sadly, "They say more about his own childishness than anything else."

Turning to gaze out the window once again, he continued, "Yes, few men would be willing to sacrifice their honour for the ones they love. But there is a God-Man that did. Not a son of Thor but the Son of God.[37] He gave Himself up for us. He is *the most wonderful thing of all* that you were waiting for – the salvation that you hoped for this Christmastide."

"That's what I've been told all my life," I sighed, "But what does it *mean*?"

"Mean?" Mr. Chesterton said quietly, continuing to stare out the window that had become heavy laden with frost. "Why, we are all in need of being saved for we cannot find ourselves. We are all lost sheep without a shepherd."

---

[37] Torvald means "Thor's ruler".

With this, he squeezed himself out the door, disappearing into the silent fury of snow. As the door shut behind him I could hear him say,

"...at night we win to the ancient inn

Where the child in the frost is furled,

We follow the feet where all souls meet

At the inn at the end of the world."[38]

Sinking lower in the chair, I buried my face in my hands. "Think, Nora! Think, Nora!" I told myself, but my mind was spent. Mr. Chesterton seemed to turn all my thoughts on their heads so that they appeared "upside down as one sees a house in a puddle."[39]

Or, has he simply turned them right side up-?

A hope flashed across my mind. *The most wonderful thing of all . . .*

---

[38] G.K. Chesterton, "The Society of Gilbert Keith Chesterton," accessed November 27, 2019, https://www.chesterton.org/a-child-of-the-snows/

[39] Chesterton, *Manalive*, 59.

A "Defence" of Armchair Philosophy

Mark Linville

One has to belong to the intelligentsia to believe things like that: no ordinary man could be such a fool.[1]

--George Orwell

Several years ago a group of leading naturalist philosophers and scientists convened a workshop titled "Moving Naturalism Forward."[2] The participants included a number of heroes of the atheistic pantheon, such as Richard Dawkins, Daniel Dennett, Owen Flanagan, and Alex Rosenberg. They

---

[1] George Orwell, "Notes on Nationalism," The Orwell Foundation, accessed November 21, 2019, https://www.orwellfoundation.com/the-orwell-foundation/orwell/essays-and-other-works/notes-on-nationalism/

[2] Sean Carroll, "Moving Naturalism Forward," YouTube, accessed November 21, 2019, https://www.youtube.com/user/seancarroll/playlists?shelf_id=3&view=50&sort=dd&view_as=subscriber.

gathered to discuss "the very difficult questions raised by replacing folk psychology and morality by a scientifically-grounded understanding of reality."

"Folk psychology" is what philosophically and scientifically untutored "folk" -- your Aunt Edna, for instance -- tend to believe about human psychology. Most people naturally think of themselves *as* selves, i.e., unified, enduring, conscious subjects of their experiences, and they believe that they have at least some measure of free will sufficient for their choices to count as their own. And they take themselves to have minds with beliefs, desires, and other 'mental contents'. "Folk morality" refers to the widespread belief that, for instance, it *really is* wrong, generally speaking, to strangle babies or to light cats ablaze for entertainment. It involves, that is, the conviction that there is a real distinction between right and wrong, good and bad, so that moral values are objective features of the world. One question of the workshop, then, is whether anything the folk believe remains once we have come to embrace a view of reality that is grounded in science. The answer to that question, according to many or most of the participants, is "Precious little." Indeed, philosopher Don Ross discussed his book, *Everything Must Go*, in which he makes it clear that he means what his title says.

A shared assumption of all of the attendees was that any scientifically untethered philosophical speculation- - especially when it appeals to anything like common sense intuitions--is worthless. Daniel Dennett did not mince words.

> I am just appalled to see how, in spite of what I think is the progress we've made in the last 25 years, there's this sort of retrograde gang ... that are going back to old-fashioned armchair philosophy of mind with relish and eagerness, and it's just sickening because their work isn't worth anything, and they lure in other people to do it. It's cute, it's clever, and it's not worth a damn.

Throwing Granny From the Train

Dennett's nausea — induced by his retrograde colleagues -- is chronic, going back decades. In 1991, he reviewed Colin McGinn's *The Problem of Consciousness*, in which McGinn argued that the problem of consciousness is essentially unsolvable by bears of little brain such as ourselves. Dennett found the claim to be "ludicrous" and "embarrassing" from the standpoint of philosophy. McGinn, it seems, "has figured out our limits from

first principles" and "without direct examination."[3]
As McGinn philosophized in his armchair, just down
the hall was a noisy band of cognitive scientists who,
by employing the new brain-imaging technologies
and computer simulations -- wholly unavailable, of
course, to either Descartes in his stove or Leibniz in
his mill -- were considering hypotheses that those
earlier philosophers would have declared to be
"inconceivable." Dennett concludes his review by
agreeing conditionally with McGinn: "Armed only
with the methods and concepts of traditional
philosophy of mind, one cannot explain
consciousness." He adds, "But we've known that for
a long time."[4] And he implies, "So much the worse
for traditional philosophy of mind."[5]

---

[3] Daniel Dennett, "Review of McGinn, The Problem of
Consciousness," Tufts University, accessed November 27,
2019, https://ase.tufts.edu/cogstud/dennett/papers/mcginn.htm.

[4] Ibid.

[5] That same year Dennett's book with the promising title
Consciousness Explained was released. But critics observed that
Dennett "explains" consciousness by explaining it away and focusing
instead upon the brain science side of the alleged equation. This led
Mary Midgley to quip, "Suggestions that Dennett should be
prosecuted for his title under the Trades Description Act are
attractive, but might call for action over too many other books to be
practicable"

Mary Midgley, *The Ethical Primate* (Abington: Routledge, 1994),
186.

In his 1991 review of a collection of essays on the work of philosopher of mind Jerry Fodor, Dennett declares that the guiding principle of all of Fodor's work is *What is good enough for Granny is good enough for Science.* That is, Fodor opposes various materialist doctrines that would "make his Granny exclaim, 'Well I never!' and lurch alarmingly in her rocker."[6] To use the language of the workshop, Granny still clings to the *Manifest Image*, which includes the common sense beliefs of Folk Psychology, and takes little or no stock in the *Scientific Image*, which precludes many of those beliefs. Of Fodor, Dennett says, "If he has to choose between Granny and science, he has made it clear that he'll choose Granny." [7]

The majority of the workshop attendees would forsake Granny for what they suppose are the clear implications of science. Indeed, Ross and Rosenberg explicitly defend *scientism*, the view that science is the "*only* way to acquire knowledge."[8] Ross complains of those philosophers who prioritize

---

[6] Daniel Dennett, "Granny's Campaign for Safe Science," Tufts University, accessed November 27, 2019, https://ase.tufts.edu/cogstud/dennett/papers/granny.htm.

[7] Ibid.

8 Alex Rosenberg, *The Atheist's Guide to Reality:Enjoying Life Without Illusions* (New York: W.W. Norton & Company, 2011), 20.

"armchair intuitions about the nature of the universe over scientific discoveries."[9] In short, neither the philosopher in his armchair nor Granny in her rocker are, in their appeal to their own common sense intuitions, likely to arrive at an even remotely accurate account of the nature of reality. Science, and science alone is our source for any knowledge of either nature or human nature, intuitions -- and Granny -- be hanged.

In this next section I lay out some of the more striking conclusions that Rosenberg draws from his commitment to a purely scientific approach to the nature of reality. I'll then turn to what I think Chesterton would say in reply. Chesterton would most certainly champion the legitimacy of an appeal to certain "first principles" in assessing the insistence that we must supplant the Manifest Image with the Scientific Image. The intended result is a Chestertonian 'defence' of armchair philosophy.

Enjoying Life With Prozac: A Formulary for Atheists

Alex Rosenberg's *The Atheist's Guide to Reality* provides us with a striking example of the view of

---

9 James Ladyman and Don Ross, *Everything Must Go: Metaphysics Naturalized* (Oxford: Oxford University Press, 2007), 10.

reality that results from "taking science seriously" -- to the point of embracing outright *scientism* -- and insisting upon a rejection of "armchair philosophy." Evidently, a commitment to scientism requires such a rejection, partly because the methodology precludes it, and partly because the resulting "scientistic" view of reality ultimately allows for the existence of neither armchairs nor philosophers.

The Atheist's Guide has the subtitle, *Enjoying Life Without Illusions*, and the "illusions" in question are the beliefs of folk morality and folk psychology. Rosenberg opens by declaring his commitment to scientism, which means "treating science as our *exclusive* guide to reality, to nature -- both our own nature and everything else's" -- which he then wields like a razor (Ockham would be proud) to slice away the illusory flesh of the Manifest Image, leaving only the bare bones of the Scientific Image. 10

One by one the illusions are dispelled. The usual suspects -- God, the soul, and immortality -- are, of course, eliminated right off the bat. Rosenberg *is* a naturalist, after all. And few will be surprised to learn that he embraces moral nihilism -- the view that there is no real difference between right and

---

[10]Rosenberg. *The Atheist's Guide to Reality*, 8. Emphasis added.

wrong. Of course, we all *believe* that there is a real difference between right and wrong, but that is an illusion "foisted off on us by our genes" so that we would behave in ways that encourage reproductive fitness. And according to Rosenberg's scientism, "physics fixes all the facts," and in a world in which this is so it is "hard to see how there could be room for moral facts."[11]

To say that physics fixes all the facts is just to say that whatever is true at the most basic physical level -- the level of fermions and bosons -- determines *everything* that is true at the higher levels, including chemistry, biology, and even human psychology. "Scientism commits us to physics as the complete description of reality,"[12] and this is to say that there is not a *smidgen* of reality that is not physical stuff abiding by physical laws. "All the processes in the universe, from atomic to bodily to mental, are purely physical processes involving fermions and bosons interacting with one another."[13]   It is physics, not turtles, all the way down, and this yields some rather disquieting results.

---

[11] Ibid., 95.

12 Rosenberg. The Atheist's Guide to Reality, 28.

13 Ibid., 21.

Bertrand Russell said that "Man is the product of causes which had no prevision of the end they were achieving."[14] It turns out that my decision to order a pizza is also the product of causes which had no prevision of the end they were achieving. The rejection of purpose or design –- teleology — at the cosmic level is a widely recognized implication of atheism.[15] But scientism implies that there is no purpose, planning, or design at *any* level, including that of the human mind. In a universe where physics fixes *all* the facts, *everything* that happens is the result of "pushes and pulls of bits of matter and fields of force,"[16] including the happenings in each brain that produce this thought or that act. Free will is an illusion. After all, the mind *just is* the brain, and the brain is physical stuff running a physical system that obeys the laws of physics and is a part of an unbroken causal chain stretching back through the natural history of the world. My thoughts and beliefs, whatever they happen to be, are the inevitable links in this chain, and they were made

---

[14] Bertrand Russell, "A Free Man's Worship," University of Notre Dame, accessed November 27, 2019, https://www3.nd.edu/~afreddos/courses/264/fmw.htm.

[15] "There is absolutely no foresight" involved in these processes." Ibid., 55.

[16] Rosenberg. The Atheist's Guide to Reality, 25.

inevitable by physical events that occurred long before any of us turned up in the universe. Our seeming conscious decisions are just "downstream effects" of prior physical processes taking place in the brain. The true causes of our thoughts and behavior are those physical processes and never our conscious choice. Scientism thus seems to entail *epiphenomenalism*, the view that there is no "mental causation." The causal arrows run only *from* the physical (e.g., the brain) *to* the mental, and never the other way around. Consciousness plays no causal role, but is more like a computer display, which merely represents, in a user friendly way, what is going on down in the machine where the real work takes place. It seems to me that I lifted the book from the shelf because I consciously *chose* to do so, but this is an illusion. What seems to be my conscious decision is the *effect* -- a user-friendly representation -- and not the *cause* of what my brain is up to. The brain is where the action is, and consciousness, one of the effects of the physical processes in the brain, is "just along for the ride."[17]

Scientism also precludes there being such a thing as the *self* in any form. Though it seems obvious to me that I have -- or *am* -- a self that is the

---

[17] Rosenberg. The Atheist's Guide to Reality, 210

subject of my experiences and the thinker of my thoughts, "The self is just another illusion."[18]   Of course, the self as an *immaterial mind* or soul is ruled out, but scientism also precludes *any* sort of unified, enduring, substantial *material* self. "There is no self in, around, or as part of anyone's body."[19] There is only the physical system that is the brain with no one there to run it. I have no more of a self than does my smartphone. All we are is fermions and bosons in the wind. There are no persons, really -- at least not in the way the folk believe. Even the private, subjective, first person point of view -- the "what-it-is-like" to be you -- is an illusion. It might seem that the experience of pain -- what some have called the "ouchiness" of pain -- eludes description with talk of tissue damage or whatever a brain scientist might observe through imaging (as regions of the brain "light up"), or observable behavior (e.g., hopping up and down, swearing, putting a smashed finger in one's mouth), but everything about your conscious experience is *in principle* describable in the third person language of neuroscience -- with no

---

[18] Rosenberg, *Atheist's Guide,* 224.

[19] Ibid., 224.

information left out. Were it not so, physics would not be the complete account of reality. [20]

Our universal idea that our thoughts are *about* stuff is also an illusion and is, in fact, the "parent" of some of the others. We do not think *about* anything, and our "thinking" is radically different from what we suppose it to be. This is because our brains are clumps of physical stuff and our thoughts are physical processes, and no one physical thing is *about* any other thing. Bananas, beets and bowling balls, being the physical stuff that they are, are never *about* anything; they just *are*. And brains, made of soggy matter, are no different. It follows that no one ever really plans or has purposes, because this would require thinking *about* the future, which is impossible. Once we see that thoughts are never about anything we will be in a better position to abandon the idea that our thoughts require a thinker -- a self -- to have them.

In fact, *nothing* is ever *about* anything -- not even the sentences that you are reading -- and therefore, nothing *means* anything, since the meaning of a statement is found in what the statement is *about*. We might have taken Rosenberg to be attempting to

---

[20] Even if current brain science is incomplete and as yet unable to provide full description.

persuade us to believe the various statements in his book to be true. But scientism precludes even this. "This book isn't conveying statements. It's rearranging neural circuits,"[21] he says, harking back to an earlier discussion of conditioning experiments on sea slugs. Through conditioning experiments, sea slugs can be taught new tricks, but it involves the release of proteins that open up channels among neurons so that other chemical molecules may pass more easily, carrying electrical charges between neurons, resulting in short-term "memory" in the slug, resulting in new habits. But the sea slug "does not learn and store any information that could be expressed in thoughts *about* stimuli." Rather, it has acquired a new habit as the result of neuronal rewiring.[22] It appears that the sort of "persuasion" in which Rosenberg is engaged is a form of conditioning, employing noises, ink marks, and pixels, aimed at the rewiring of his readers' circuitry, resulting in the acquisition of new behavioral habits of mind -- i.e., brain -- that the folk would call "being persuaded that scientism is true." This reading of Rosenberg is reinforced by his discussion of the difference between his preferred therapy – drugs --

---

[21] Rosenberg, The Atheist's Guide to Reality, 193.

[22] Ibid., 182.

and "talk therapy." If the latter works at all, it does so through rearranging brain circuitry literally as the result of words as emitted sounds and their behavioral associations, but not because of their propositional content.

> Your therapist talks to you. The acoustical vibrations from your therapist's mouth to your ear starts a chain of neurons firing in the brain. Together with the circuits already set to fire in your brain, the result is some changes somewhere inside your head.[23]

This appears to be *persuasion naturalized*, so that philosophical conversion, as happens when one comes to be "convinced" by argument, is not essentially different from neuronal changes that may be effected through chemicals. Convincing readers to embrace scientism is much like teaching new tricks to sea slugs.

Rosenberg knows that the picture he paints of reality and our place in it is bleak -- depressing, even -- and quite literally disillusioning. Human existence has no meaning or purpose, and human life has no intrinsic value. Death has the final word. Morality is an illusion. There is no free will or even

---

[23] Rosenberg, The Atheist's Guide to Reality, 285.

any sort of self to enjoy it. We are simply pushed along by impersonal physical forces beyond our control. We are deceived when we think that we have purposes and plans that we carry out. Even love, which seems to give so much meaning to life is not what we have supposed it to be, but is merely an evolutionary adaptation -- an "irrational" one at that -- selected for the role it plays in ensuring and increasing reproductive fitness.

That's a lot of disillusionment packed between the covers of one book. And so Rosenberg closes with this advice: "Take a Prozac or your favorite serotonin reuptake inhibitor, and keep taking them until they kick in."[24]

The Preternaturally Stupid Pretensions of Scientism

G.K. Chesterton quipped that it was not the arguments of Christian apologetics that nudged him away from his paganism and agnosticism and in the direction of Christianity. Rather, it was the "scientific and sceptical literature" of his day. "As I laid down the last of Colonel Ingersoll's atheistic lectures the dreadful thought broke across my mind,

---

[24] Rosenberg, The Atheist's Guide to Reality, 315.

'Almost thou persuadest me to be a Christian.'"[25] Had Alex Rosenberg's work been available to the young and inquisitive Chesterton, the effect might have been magnified; he might have taken a vow of poverty or entered a monastery or even mounted a pillar and achieved historical fame under the name Gilbert the Stylite. The older and wiser Chesterton would have regarded *The Atheist's Guide* as the ravings of a mind grown morbid.

Rosenberg espouses many "heresies" that would have earned him at least a chapter in Chesterton's *Heretics*. He embraces moral nihilism, and declares that there is no real difference between right and wrong. Yet Chesterton recognized the precept, "Babies should not be strangled" as a "mystical dogma" -- *mystical* because it is neither established nor impugned by reason, but known immediately -- and *dogma* because it is a settled and authoritative truth. Rosenberg insists that the self is an illusion, to which Chesterton would reply, "You cannot call up any wilder vision than a city in which men ask themselves if they have any selves."[26] To Rosenberg's insistence that "Scientism commits us

---

[25] G.K. Chesterton, *Orthodoxy* in *The Collected Works of G.K. Chesterton,* vol. 1 (San Francisco: Ignatius Press, 1986), 288.

[26] Chesterton, *Orthodoxy,* 240.

to physics as the complete description of reality," Chesterton might reply, "The madman's explanation of a thing is always complete."[27] The madman who insists that he is the King of England is not hindered by the observation that the King is on his throne and revered by the nation. This, you see, is all a part of the plot against him. *All* seemingly contrary evidence is assimilated into his mad theory.

Where Rosenberg insists that free will is an illusion and that our every thought and deed is the inevitable outcome of a "chain of prior events," Chesterton would observe that, "It is the worst chain that ever fettered a human being."[28] The man who "disbelieves in the reality of the will" is not even free to "say 'Thank you' for the mustard."[29] How much less is he free to expect his readers to weigh the arguments in his book, to deliberate, and offer a rational assessment of their merits? If my every thought is an inevitable link in a chain of physical events stretching back into and beyond a dim and prehistoric past, then whatever verdict I reach was already in the cards before Adam took to wearing fig leaves. For every thought and every act, "We are

---

[27] Chesterton, *Orthodoxy,* 222.

[28] Ibid., 228.

[29] Ibid.

either unable to do things or we are destined to do them."[30] If I am unpersuaded by Rosenberg's arguments, well, then, whatever 'reasoning' led me to my conclusion cannot have been up to me. "Nothing was up to me. Everything--including my choice and my feeling that I can choose freely--was fixed by earlier states of the universe plus the laws of physics."[31] But then neither was the writing of *The Atheist's Guide* up to the author. Each and every sentence that wound up on those pages was chosen -- by no one -- before the foundation of the world. The thoughts in Rosenberg's brain are the products of configurations of physical stuff that was once the stuff of stars. Each molecule had an appointment with destiny, to be in precisely *that* configuration to give rise to precisely *that* thought just as surely as the various travelers were each predestined to gather on the *Bridge of San Luis Rey*.

Rosenberg insists that the physical universe is "causally closed" and that "we are all just a part of a physical universe." Chesterton would reply that if so, then it is also *locked*, like a vast cosmic prison, and "the machinery of this cosmic prison is something

---

[30] Chesterton, *Orthodoxy*, 265. I have altered the tense of the original sentence.

[31] Rosenberg, *The Atheist's Guide*, 236.

that cannot be broken; for we ourselves are only a part of its machinery" and "if the mind is mechanical, thought cannot be very exciting."[32] One might add that if the mind is mechanical and operates as it does because its own gears are engaged with the "omnipotent but blind" machinery of the physical universe, then the mechanism ultimately responsible for my beliefs would appear to be quite indifferent to the matter of whether those beliefs are *true*.[33] Rosenberg's universe is a prison "empty of all that is human,"[34] and this includes human reason.

To Rosenberg's repeated insistence that our thoughts are never *about* anything, Chesterton might reply, "There is a thought that stops thought. That is the only thought that ought to be stopped."[35] If our thoughts are not *about* anything, then they are not thoughts, for *aboutness* is essential to thinking. If our thoughts are never about anything then we never *believe* (or *dis*believe) anything -- such as the many seeming assertions in Rosenberg's book -- for

---

32 Chesterton, *Orthodoxy*, 265.

33 Bertrand Russell's language in "A Free Man's Worship". See Bertrand Russell, *Why I Am Not a Christian And Other Essays on Religion and Related Subjects* (New York: Simon and Schuster, 1957), 108.

34 Chesterton, *Orthodoxy*, 265.

35 Ibid.,236

beliefs are essentially about propositions and what they say about reality. It is a good thing, then, that Rosenberg tells us that he is not saying anything that he wishes us to believe. His claim that the book does not convey *statements* amounts to the claim that the sentences -- the black squiggly characters on the pages -- do not express *propositions*.[36] But all and only propositions have *truth value*, which is to say that all and only propositions are *either true or false*. And so Rosenberg tells his reader, in effect, that the apparent claims made in his book are *neither true nor false*. We might imagine Chesterton replying, "Well, then, it follows that nothing said in your book is *true*." And he would be right. But then why should the reader submit his brain to Rosenberg's efforts at "neuronal rewiring" if the result is not a matter of replacing false beliefs with true ones? In fact, it is hard to see how Rosenberg has left himself with the resources for telling us it is *true* that "Physics fixes the facts" because this would amount to saying that that proposition describes the way the world actually is. But this requires that the proposition be *about* the world, and we have been assured that nothing is ever about anything. In the

---

[36] "Statement" and "proposition" are synonymous--or treated as such by Rosenberg. See p. 192.

immediate vicinity of his statement that he is not making statements, he avoids speaking of "true" or "false" beliefs and instead speaks of "accurate" and "inaccurate" information. But even *that* language seems to require that the "information" be *about* stuff so that it either accurately or inaccurately represents things as they really are. What else can it mean? (And elsewhere throughout the book he lapses into folksy talk of true and false beliefs.)

So far, we have seen reason for thinking that Rosenberg's scientism leaves no room for rational deliberation, beliefs, propositions, or even truth. Scientism is indeed a "thought that stops thought." One of Rosenberg's concerns is to "close down the wiggle room"[37] that would allow for "compromises with theism." He writes, "If Darwinian biology allows a few exceptions, it won't be able to keep the floodgates closed against intelligent design, special creation, or even biblical inerrancy."[38]   In his discussion of "The Suicide of Thought," Chesterton observes,

> In the act of destroying the idea of Divine authority we have largely destroyed the idea of that human authority by which we do a long-division sum. With a long and

---

[37]Rosenberg, *Atheist's Guide*, 53.
[38] Ibid., 53.

sustained tug we have attempted to pull
the mitre off pontifical man; and his head
has come off with it.[39]

Now, all of these untoward conclusions are the
natural fruit of scientism. Why, then, embrace
scientism? Rosenberg's answer, put variously
throughout his book, is the success story of science
as physics over the last several centuries.

> The phenomenal accuracy of its
> prediction, the unimaginable power of its
> technological application, and the
> breathtaking extent and detail of its
> explanations are powerful reasons to
> believe that physics is the whole truth
> about reality.[40]

He appeals to this success as a way of dismissing
arguments to the contrary as they have been offered
by mere armchair philosophers, such as Descartes.
"Even before you hear them, science provides a
compelling argument that they must be all wrong.
One has only to weigh the evidence for scientism --
500 years of scientific progress -- and the evidence

---

[39] Chesterton, *Orthodoxy,* 237.

[40] Rosenberg, *Atheist's Guide,* 25.

against it -- including those cute conundrums. It's clear which side has the weightier evidence."[41]

Now we might *see* Rosenberg's 500 years of scientific success and *raise* him 50,000 years of human consciousness of the sort that his scientism denies. Rosenberg's assurances to his readers that the first-person experiences that they are having -- even as they are reading him -- are not real is reminiscent of "Baghdad Bob" -- the Iraqi Information Minister who, in 2003, assured the international press that U.S. forces were nowhere near Baghdad, even as U.S. tanks were seen just over his shoulder.

In the Q & A portion of his debate with William Lane Craig, Rosenberg was asked whether his claim that "sentences have no meaning" was just incoherent. He prefaced his answer with, "I ain't so stupid as to contradict myself in the puerile way that you are suggesting." Had Chesterton been present, he might kindly have ventured a different opinion.

> That same suppression of sympathies, that same waving away of intuitions or guess-work which make a man preternaturally clever in dealing with the stomach of a spider, will make him

---

[41] Rosenberg, *Atheist's Guide*, 227.

preternaturally stupid in dealing with the heart of man. He is making himself inhuman in order to understand humanity.[42]

Here is Chesterton's direct challenge to scientism as well as to the standard defense of scientism. Our scientistic philosopher reasons that physicalist assumptions and the scientific method have worked so well for understanding the digestive functions of arachnids that it is a seamless move to apply those same assumptions and methods in seeking to understand the wellsprings of human thought and emotion. Yes. And because the pressure washer has worked so well on the siding, the deck, and the driveway, we should also use it for cleaning out the dog's ears. As they say, to the man with a Large Hadron Collider everything looks like a proton.

One might imagine Chesterton updating his examples to involve Rosenberg's sea slugs, as the move from mollusks to minds runs along the same rails as inferences from the inner workings of spider stomachs to the inner workings of poets and philosophers.

---

[42] G.K. Chesterton, Heretics in G.K. Chesterton: Collected Works, vol. 1, 115.

> A man can understand astronomy only by being an astronomer; he can understand entomology only by being an entomologist (or, perhaps, an insect); but he can understand a great deal of anthropology merely by being a man. He is himself the animal which he studies.[43]

As such, the anthropologist -- who is also an ἄνθρωπος[44] -- is capable of studying himself from the inside out. Perhaps this is why Chesterton once observed, "I prefer even the fancies and prejudices of the people who see life from the inside to the clearest demonstrations of the people who see life from the outside."[45] Tell the regulars at The Drunken Duck that there is no such thing as "what-it-is-like" to be themselves, that they never think *about* anything, and that they never make plans--and that this is because your theory of reality does not permit it -- and they may reply that, having thought *about* such claims, there is such a thing as "what-it-is-like" to think that you are an idiot, and you should plan to go back to where you came from. And they will have the advantage of the argument.

---

[43] Chesterton, *Heretics. 115.*

[44] Anthropos, i.e., human being.

[45] Chesterton, *Orthodoxy* (elfland)

Unless his mind has been fettered by an ideology like scientism, our anthropologist has immediate and privileged access to the most relevant data for theory construction, i.e., the data of his own conscious experience. He will see that the assumption that human thought is the same *kind* of thing as 'thought' in sea slugs -- so that we must deny everything of the former that is denied of the latter -- is absurd. And he will regard the suggestion that we must abandon those very features of human cognition that are essential for doing science -- and that we must do so *in the name of* science -- as incoherent.

Our argument is not that we are warranted in rejecting just any scientific claim that strikes us as "counterintuitive." Recall that the entomologist is "preternaturally clever" partly because he waves intuitions away and does science. H.G. Wells observed,

> The universe at that plane to which the mind of the molecular physicist descends has none of the shapes or forms of our common life whatever. This hand with which I write is in the universe of molecular physics a cloud of warring atoms and molecules, combining and recombining, colliding, rotating, flying

hither and thither in the universal atmosphere of ether.[46]

Who would have thought that a punch in the nose resembles a collision of galaxies? Chesterton took exception to much that Wells said in that paper, but not to this. The world may be stranger than common sense alone may have led us to guess, but common sense learns to accommodate such unexpected facts. And common sense bows to science, not to the a priori deductions of the armchair philosopher, as our means of learning the nature of the physical world -- so long as the claims of science stay within the lines of logical coherence. Chesterton's objection was to Wells' central thesis, namely, that we cannot trust our reason -- "the instrument" -- as a reliable guide to truth. Common sense can no more accommodate this claim than it can accommodate married bachelors, for the claim is incoherent, as are the several claims of scientism.

Chesterton was emphatic that with humanity something *qualitatively* different from the rest of the natural world arrived on the scene. "It is not natural to see man as a natural product. It is not common sense to call man a common object of the

---

[46] H.G. Wells, "Scepticism of the Instrument," *Mind*, vol. xiii. (New Series), No. 51.

country or the seashore. It is not seeing straight to see him as an animal. It is not sane."[47] It is not seeing man "as he is" when seen in the broad daylight, "the solid thing standing in the sunlight," and not through the lens of some theory. He imagines an alien mind coming to observe the natural -- non-human - -world for the first time, and declares that such a mind would be wholly unprepared for the first man. [48] Just as he was beginning to think that one species shades off imperceptibly to the next, he would be startled by this wholly new thing. It would be "like seeing one cow out of a hundred cows suddenly jump over the moon or one pig out of a hundred pigs grow wings in a flash and fly."[49] "Man is not merely an evolution but a revolution."[50] "The more we look at man as an animal, the less he will look like one."[51] We have found prehistoric cave art where an early ancestor used ochre to draw reindeer. But we have yet to find a place where a reindeer had drawn a picture of a man.[52] Of these

---

[47] G.K. Chesterton, *The Everlasting Man* in *G.K. Chesterton: Collected Works* (San Francisco: Ignatius Press, 1986), p. 168.

[48] Ibid.

[49] Ibid., 169.

[50] Ibid., 158.

[51] Ibid., 159.

[52] Chesterton, *The Everlasting Man*. 165.

primeval and subterranean masterpieces, Chesterton observes that "Art is the signature of man."[53] We might amend this by noting that the arts *and sciences* are the signature of man, for we are gifted with both imagination and reason that have no precedent -- not even in sea slugs.

Materialists and Madmen

Chesterton adds that this, i.e., the startling uniqueness and qualitative difference between beast and man, "is the sort of simple truth with which a story of beginnings ought really to begin."[54] Having begun there we shall refuse any theory that denies the clear facts for the sake of its own consistency. This is armchair philosophy at its finest. If we keep this image of humanity -- man the artist, man the dreamer, man the comedian who, "alone among the animals ... is shaken with the beautiful madness called laughter,"[55] man the logician and metaphysician -- fixed before our eyes and then attempt to explain him, then we shall have a wild tale to tell. "He seems rather more supernatural as a natural product than as a

---

[53] Chesterton, *The Everlasting Man,* 166.
[54] Ibid.
[55] Ibid., 168.

supernatural one."[56] It is no wonder -- or perhaps it was with great wonder -- that Bertrand Russell observed that it was "a strange mystery" that nature has "brought forth at last a child ... gifted with sight, with knowledge of good and evil, with the capacity of judging all the works of his unthinking mother."[57] Scientism would seek to diminish the mystery by downplaying the strangeness. This way lies madness.

It is often said that the madman is the man who has lost his reason. But Chesterton insists that the madman is the man who has lost everything *except* his reason.[58] What he means is that the madman begins with a view of things that defies the obvious, such as P.G. Wodehouse's Duke of Ramfurline, who is "under the impression — this is in the strictest confidence — that he is a canary,"[59] and then is *relentless* in carrying out all of the logical and practical implications of the axiom. This, of course, would explain the cuttlebone, the swinging perch, and the merry whistling at sunrise. His reason is not

---

[56] Chesterton, *The Everlasting Man.* 165.

[57] Russell, *Why I Am Not a Christian.* 107.

[58] Chesterton, *Orthodoxy,* 222.

[59] P.G. Wodehouse, *The Inimitable Jeeves* (New York: Harry N. Abrams, 2007).

the problem. He is a perfect Spinozan in deducing the cuttlebone. It is his starting point that is off.

> Now, speaking quite externally and empirically, we may say that the strongest and most unmistakable *mark* of madness is this combination between a logical completeness and a piritual contraction. The lunatic's theory explains a large number of things, but it does not explain them in a large way.[60]

The trouble is that he is "in the clean and well-lit prison of one idea,"[61] and it is a prison without windows that would permit him to see the world as it is in the light of day. He has employed his reason well enough, taking that "one idea" and explaining *everything* in its light, but it is "reason without root, reason in the void." He has gone mad because he has begun his thinking "without the proper first principles," and these are the principles of Common Sense.

An example of the sort of belief that arises from proper first principles is "I am a man and not a canary." Another one is "Babies should not be strangled." Yet another is "I have first-person

---

[60] Chesterton, *Orthodoxy*, 222.

[61] Ibid., 225.

conscious experiences." Still another is, "I sometimes think about stuff." Chesterton discerns this same "reason in the void," this same prison of one idea in various ideologies or philosophical theories, such as materialism. As a theory it shares with madness that same combination of "an expansive and exhaustive reason with a contracted common sense."[62] It is exhaustive in that it pretends to explain *everything*. It is contracted in its fixation on "one thin idea" as the complete explanation. As such it has "a sort of insane simplicity. It has just the quality of the madman's argument; we have at once the sense of it covering everything and the sense of it leaving everything out."[63]

> His cosmos may be complete in every rivet and cog-wheel, but still his cosmos is smaller than our world. Somehow his scheme, like the lucid scheme of the madman, seems unconscious of the alien energies and the large indifference of the earth; it is not thinking of the real things of the earth, of fighting peoples or proud mothers, or first love or fear upon the sea.[64]

---

[62] Chesterton, *Orthodoxy*. 225.

[63] Ibid.

[64] Ibid.

Rosenberg's scientism leads him to latch on to the idea that "physics fixes all the facts," and he is quite sure that physics tells the *complete* story of all of reality. He is a materialist -- like Chesterton's materialist -- but his resulting view of reality is madness -- like Chesterton's maniac. He has made himself inhuman in order to understand humanity, and he has done so by insisting that physics and physics alone explains *everything* and then casting aside anything that physics cannot, in principle, explain. Those who insist that reality includes such things as selves, each with their own first-person point of view (and that this is obvious to each of us), he deems "mystery mongers." But Chesterton observes that "Mysticism keeps men sane." This is because there are things that we know without demonstration, and these the healthy man embraces as First Principles. And it is only with these laid down as bedrock that demonstration, including scientific demonstration, begins.

> The whole secret of mysticism is this: that man can understand everything by the help of what he does not understand. The morbid logician seeks to make everything lucid, and succeeds in making everything mysterious. The mystic allows one thing

to be mysterious, and everything else becomes lucid.[65]

Scientism is an especially striking example of "reason without root," and it is madness.

Rosenberg recommends Prozac to his readers in order to counter the complications from embracing scientism. Chesterton prescribes a much more "desperate remedy." In dealing with the madman, who thinks he is a canary or that his head is a pumpkin, doctors and psychologists are "profoundly intolerant."

> Their attitude is really this: that the man must stop thinking, if he is to go on living. Their counsel is one of intellectual amputation.[66]

> "There is a thought that stops thought. That is the only thought that ought to be stopped," he has said. If your project is wrongheaded--having the wrong head or starting assumptions--and if a wholesale rejection of the Manifest Image results in manifest absurdities, scrap it for something more likely to allow you to see

---

[65] Chesterton, *Orthodoxy*, 231.
[66] Ibid., 224.

things as they are. 'If thy *head* offend thee, cut it off.'[67]

---

[67] Chesterton, *Orthodoxy*, 224.

CHESTERTON AS PHILOSOPHER: THE REVIVAL OF PHILOSOPHY

G.K. Chesterton

From *The Common Man*: "The best reason for a revival of philosophy is that unless a man has a philosophy certain horrible things will happen to him. He will be practical; he will be progressive; he will cultivate efficiency; he will trust in evolution; he will do the work that lies nearest; he will devote himself to deeds, not words. Thus struck down by blow after blow of blind stupidity and random fate, he will stagger on to a miserable death with no comfort but a series of catchwords; such as those which I have catalogued above. Those things are simply substitutes for thoughts. In some cases they are the tags and tail-ends of somebody else's thinking. That means that a man who refuses to have his own philosophy will not even have the advantages of a brute beast, and be left to his own instincts. He will only have the used-up scraps of somebody else's philosophy; which the beasts do not have to inherit; hence their happiness. Men have always one of two things: either a complete and conscious philosophy or the unconscious acceptance of the broken bits of some incomplete and shattered and often discredited philosophy. Such broken bits are the phrases I have quoted: efficiency and evolution and the rest. The idea of being "practical", standing all by itself, is all that remains of a Pragmatism that cannot stand at all. It is impossible to be practical without a Pragma. And what would happen if you went up to the next practical man you met and said to the poor dear old duffer, "Where is your Pragma?" Doing the work that is nearest is obvious nonsense; yet it has been repeated in many albums. In nine cases out of ten it would mean doing the work that we are least fitted to do, such as cleaning the windows or clouting the policeman over the head. "Deeds, not words" is itself an excellent example of "Words, not thoughts." It is a deed to throw a pebble into a pond and a word that sends a prisoner to the gallows. But there are certainly very futile words; and this sort of journalistic philosophy and popular science almost entirely consists of them.

Some people fear that philosophy will bore or bewilder them; because they think it is not only a string of long words, but a tangle of complicated notions. These people miss the whole point of the modern situation. These are exactly the evils that exist already; mostly for want of a philosophy. The politicians and the papers are always using long words. It is not a complete consolation that they use them wrong. The political and social relations are already hopelessly complicated. They are far more complicated than any page of medieval metaphysics; the only difference is that the medievalist could trace out the tangle and follow the complications; and the moderns cannot. The chief practical things of today, like finance and political corruption, are frightfully complicated. We are content to tolerate them because we are content to misunderstand them, not to understand them. The business world needs metaphysics – to simplify it.

I know these words will be received with scorn, and with gruff reassertion that this is no time for nonsense and paradox; and that what is really wanted is a practical man to go in and clear up the mess. And a practical man will doubtless appear, one of the unending succession of practical men; and he will doubtless go in, and perhaps clear up a few millions for himself and leave the mess more bewildering than before; as each of the other practical men has done. The reason is perfectly simple. This sort of rather crude and unconscious person always adds to the confusion; because lie himself has two or three different motives at the same moment, and does not distinguish between them. A man has, already entangled hopelessly in his own mind, (1) a hearty and human desire for money, (2) a somewhat priggish and superficial desire to be progressing, or going the way the world is going, (3) a dislike to being thought too old to keep up with the young people, (4) a certain amount of vague but genuine patriotism or public spirit, (5) a misunderstanding of a mistake made by Mr. H. G. Wells, in the form of a book on Evolution. When a man has all these things in his head, and does not even attempt to sort them out, he is called by common consent and acclamation a practical man. But the practical man cannot be expected to improve the impracticable muddle; for he cannot clear up the muddle in his own mind, let alone in his own highly complex community and civilisation. For some strange reason, it is the custom to say of this sort of practical man that "he knows his own mind". Of course this is exactly what he does not know. He may in a few fortunate cases know what he wants, as does a dog or a baby of two years old; but even then he does not know why he wants it. And it is the why and the how that have to be considered when we are tracing out the way in which some culture or tradition has got into a tangle. What we need, as the ancients understood, is not a politician who is a business man, but a king who is a philosopher.

I apologise for the word "king," which is not strictly necessary to the sense; but I suggest that it would be one of the functions of the philosopher to pause upon such words, and determine their importance and unimportance. The Roman Republic and all its citizens had to the last a horror of the word "king". It was in consequence of this that they invented and imposed on us the word "Emperor." The great Republicans who founded America also had a horror of the word "king;" which has therefore reappeared with the special qualification of a Steel King, an Oil King, a Pork King, or other similar monarchs made of similar materials. The business of the philosopher is not necessarily to condemn the innovation or to deny the distinction. But it is his duty to ask himself exactly what it is that he or others dislike in the word "king." If what he dislikes is a man wearing the spotted fur of a small animal called the ermine, or a man having once had a metal ring placed on the top of his head by a clergyman, he will decide one way. If what he dislikes is a man having vast or irresponsible powers over other men, he may decide another. If what he dislikes is such fur or such power being handed on from father to son, he will enquire whether this ever occurs under commercial conditions today. But, anyhow, he will have the habit of testing the thing by the thought; by the idea which he likes or dislikes; and not merely by the sound of a syllable or the look of four letters beginning with a "R."

Philosophy is merely thought that has been thought out. It is often a great bore. But man has no alternative, except between being influenced by thought that has been thought out and being influenced by thought that has not been thought out. The latter is what we commonly call culture and enlightenment today. But man is always influenced by thought of some kind, his own or somebody else's; that of somebody he trusts or that of somebody he never heard of, thought at first, second or third hand; thought from exploded legends or unverified rumours; but always something with the shadow of a system of values and a reason for preference. A man does test everything by something. The question here is whether he has ever tested the test.

I will take one example out of a thousand that might be taken. What is the attitude of an ordinary man on being told of an extraordinary event: a miracle? I mean the sort of thing that is loosely called supernatural, but should more properly be called preternatural. For the word supernatural applies only to what is higher than man; and a good many modern miracles look as if they came from what is considerably lower. Anyhow, what do modern men say when apparently confronted -with something that cannot, in the cant phrase, be naturally explained? Well, most modern men immediately talk nonsense. When such a thing is currently mentioned, in novels or newspapers or magazine stories, the first comment is always something like, "But my dear fellow, this is the twentieth century!" It is worth having a little training in philosophy if only to avoid looking so ghastly a fool as that. It has on the whole rather less sense or meaning than saying, "But my dear fellow, this is Tuesday afternoon." If miracles cannot happen, they cannot happen in the twentieth century or in the twelfth. If they can happen, nobody can prove that there is a time when they cannot happen. The best that can be said for the sceptic is that he cannot say what he means, and therefore, whatever else he means, he cannot mean what he says. But if he only means that miracles can be <believed> in the twelfth century, but cannot be believed in the twentieth, then he is wrong again, both in theory and in fact. He is wrong in theory, because an intelligent recognition of possibilities does not depend on a date but on a philosophy. An atheist could disbelieve in the first century and a mystic could continue to believe in the twenty-first century. And he is wrong, in fact, because there is every sign of there being a great deal of mysticism and miracle in the twenty-first century; and there is quite certainly an increasing mass of it in the twentieth.

But I have only taken that first superficial repartee because there is a significance in the mere fact that it comes first; and its very superficiality reveals something of the subconsciousness. It is almost an automatic repartee; and automatic words are of some importance in psychology. Let us not be too severe on the worthy gentleman who informs his dear fellow that it is the twentieth century. In the mysterious depths of his being even that enormous ass does actually mean something. The point is that he cannot really explain what he means; and <that> is the argument for a better education in philosophy. What he really means is something like this, "There is a theory of this mysterious universe to which more and more people were in fact inclined during the second half of the eighteenth and the first half of the nineteenth centuries; and up to that point at least, this theory did grow with the growing inventions and discoveries of science to which we owe our present social organisation – or disorganisation. That theory maintains that cause and effect have from the first operated in an uninterrupted sequence like a fixed fate; and that there is no will behind or within that fate; so that it must work itself out in the absence of such a will, as a machine must run down in the absence of a man. There were more people in the nineteenth century than in the ninth who happened to hold this particular theory of the universe. I myself happened to hold it; and therefore I obviously cannot believe in miracles." That is perfectly good sense; but so is the counter-statement; "I do not happen to hold it; and therefore I obviously can believe in miracles."

The advantage of an elementary philosophic habit is that it permits a man, for instance, to understand a statement like this, Whether there can or can not be exceptions to a process depends on the nature of that process." The disadvantage of not having it is that a man will turn impatiently even from so simple a truism; and call it metaphysical gibberish. He will then go off and say: "One can't have such things in the twentieth century"; which really is gibberish. Yet the former statement could surely be explained to him in sufficiently simple terms. If a man sees a river run downhill day after day and year after year, he is justified in reckoning, we might say in betting, that it will do so till he dies. But he is not justified in saying that it cannot run uphill, until he really knows why it runs downhill. To say it does so by gravitation answers the physical but not the philosophical question. It only repeats that there is a repetition; it does not touch the deeper question of whether that repetition could be altered by anything outside it. And that depends on whether there <is> anything outside it. For instance, suppose that a man had only seen the river in a dream. He might have seen it in a hundred dreams, always repeating itself and always running downhill. But that would not prevent the hundredth dream being different and the river climbing the mountain; because the dream is a dream, and there <is> something outside it. Mere repetition does not prove reality or inevitability. We must know the nature of the thing and the cause of the repetition. If the nature of the thing is a Creation, and the cause of the thing a Creator, in other words if the repetition itself is only the repetition of something willed by a person, then it is <not> impossible for the same person to will a different thing. If a man is a fool for believing in a Creator, then he is a fool for believing in a miracle; but not otherwise. Otherwise, he is simply a philosopher who is consistent in his philosophy.

A modern man is quite free to choose either philosophy. But what is actually the matter with the modern man is that he does not know even his own philosophy; but only his own phraseology. He can only answer the next spiritual message produced by a spiritualist, or the next cure attested by doctors at Lourdes, by repeating what are generally nothing but phrases; or are, at their best, prejudices.

Thus, when so brilliant a man as Mr. H. G. Wells says that such supernatural ideas have become impossible "for intelligent people ", he is (for that instant) not talking like an intelligent person. In other words, he is not talking like a philosopher; because he is not even saying what he means. What he means is, not "impossible for intelligent men," but, "impossible for intelligent monists," or, "impossible for intelligent determinists." But it is not a negation of <intelligence> to hold any coherent and logical conception of so mysterious a world. It is not a negation of intelligence to think that all experience is a dream. It is not unintelligent to think it a delusion, as some Buddhists do; let alone to think it a product of creative will, as Christians do. We are always being told that men must no longer be so sharply divided into their different religions.

As an immediate step in progress, it is much more urgent that they should be more clearly and more sharply divided into their different philosophies.

ANOTHER RESURRECTION: IF ONLY WE COULD UNDERSTAND

Donald W. Catchings, Jr.

G. K. Chesterton's *The Everlasting Man* is a beautiful, engaging, and insightful summary of human history understood from the perspective of Christ's Church. In this work, Chesterton displays two very important elements of history that have been overlooked in modern society. First, mankind is so much more than modern society imagines — an artist made in the image of the original, Everlasting Artist. Second, Christ is so much more than the world is willing to see. He is the inevitable goal of human imagination and reason; the only place in which both can coexist — that is, find their true place. If we could grasp what this work is demanding of us, we could again resurrect the Gospel and the Church's power over society. We could pull Post-Modern Man from the Dark Age (Cave) that avails him.

Another Resurrection: If Only We Could Understand

If only we could understand
The Everlasting Man.
    If only we could see
    What it means to be
'   The Creature Called Man.'

No, not that brutish fable,
Shallow-browed, dragging knuckles.
    Waiting in the cave's dim light
    Is this Creature's tell-tale sign
    That he is the measuring rod,
    The little-world and Image of
    The Everlasting God.

An artist, through and through,
And as record proves, "civilized" too.[1]
    At the dawn of history's pages,
    Filled with Golden Ages,
    The Creature stands erect,

---

[1] G.K. Chesterton, *The Everlasting Man* (San Francisco: Ignatius Press, 2008), 56.

As nature resurrects,
With piety intact.

He worships the rise and fall
Of sun and crops with a zealous song.
    Religious and traditional.
    Not a mere animal.
    Not a link to the past.
    He is more than that.
    May we see at last . . .

When rhythms dance—riddle and rhyme;
Those dreams in the Creature's spiritual mind.
    Creative light reflects in song,
    The truth myth sang all along:
    Behind the veiled, mysterious lands,
    Beyond visible history stands
    The Everlasting Hands.

With imagination he rightly sees
The most reasonable of imaginings:
    Reason is a Being;
    A Being with imagining.
    There are signs in the starry-hosts.
    There is a story in the cosmos—
    This he surely knows.

And with reason, he is able
To imagine the most reasonable:
    Imagination is the beginning
    Of all thinking beings.
    There is more than the shadow.
    There is an everlasting glow
    Beyond all he knows.

In his spirit, a hunger is seen
For that which is food for the hungry being:
    More than myth-making
    Or strength-seeking;
    More than the sage's wise words
    Or the sacrificed herds—
    A voice is heard.

On progress's path, a dark split comes;
A new hunger rises to tempt their taste buds.
    In "Tyre and Sidon,"
    A "short cut" is come upon.[2]
    Unlocking the door to Shame-King
    With evil's strengthening key,
    Philosophy's enemy.

Not a trifle on the Creature's path,

---

[2] Chesterton, *The Everlasting Man,* 123.

This evil way that was conquered at last:
>Though overcome by good,
>Not overcome for good;
>For as time moves ever-forward,
>A new challenge is offered
>That withers the sacred.

Thoughts and not-thoughts, leading to death,
For the Creature sees the gods were always dead.
>Vehemence and indifference stand,
>A heavy stone for faithless man.
>A new war, though old, must be won,
>As the end of Old World comes,
>By the Everlasting Man.

If only we could understand
The Everlasting Man.
>If only we could see
>With our fleshly eyes
>'The Man Called Christ.'

Out of the cave, a child they bring—
The truer, the greater Philosopher-King.
>The infant artist of the cosmos;
>The tender shoot of starry hosts;
>The Shepherd of every field,
>Worshipped while groping for milk,

Attacked while swaddled in linen still.

Here the great parable riddles in rhyme,
That terrible mercy that echoes through time.
  Answered in doctrine.
  Clear in tradition.
  Walking in dewy dawn—
  The foreseen, Resurrected One—
  Bringing Life back to live in a new garden.

Strange, this story told about the Man
Who brought back keys from the devil's own hand.
  Keys to unlock a holy door,
  Inside, a rock giving foundation for
  A movement to move civil men
  Past their weak and heretical strand
  Onto the firm truth that converts the pagan.

Mighty hands and arms outstretched,
Through children born of His faithfulness.
  The Christ calls together at last
  Spirit and reason to break the past
  Chains of fools in the dark
  With force of peace or holy war
  To deliver from false stories, the world.

Alive at last and living in liberty,

Calling all peoples to finally be free.
> In Christ and His Church
> The romantic truth bursts
> On reserved lines,
> Creating new, mankind—
> Giving all the chance of a new mind.

Unique to this Man, unique to His house,
Life from death everlastingly aroused.
> Conquering death, grave, hell:
> Overcoming the despair of self,
> The Body does rise—
> The Church and the Christ—
> Rushing against rivers, turning back time.

The Everlasting Man and His Everlasting Bride
Continue to rise, to history's surprise.
> This turn, never to be conquered.
> This Christ, more than a brother,
> A God too—
> The Everlasting Truth,
> Never to die, Ever to move.

If only we could understand
The Everlasting Man.
　　If only we could see
　　What it means to be
　　The Post-Modern Man.

CREATION, CORRUPTION, AND CELEBRATION ON A THURSDAY

Shawn White

If you are a student of the Christian worldview, then you are probably familiar with the theme of Creation, Fall, and Restoration. Depending on who you read, some might also include Redemption in between Fall and Restoration. For this essay and the purposes of alliteration, I am going to use the terms Creation, Corruption, and Celebration in speaking about G.K. Chesterton's novel *The Man Who Was Thursday: A Nightmare.*[1] It is necessary to state upfront that this essay will not provide an exhaustive examination of each of three motifs (and there are more besides these three). A thorough

---

[1] G.K. Chesterton, *The Man Who Was Thursday: A Nightmare*, (San Francisco, CA: Ignatius Press, 1999). I will be using this version of the book exclusively throughout this essay.

analysis would require a much more extended treatment of Chesterton's novel, perhaps a book in itself. The best that can be done in the space allotted is a brief sketch of each motif to allow the reader of this novel to see these themes a bit more clearly.

The Man Who Was Thursday: A Nightmare is an exciting book solely on its surface. It is full of wild scenes, some that perhaps feel disjointed from time to time in their juxtaposition. It is a fast-paced detective story centered around the cat-and-mouse game of the anarchists and the Scotland Yard detectives who are determined to stop an assassination via bombing of a foreign dignitary on French soil. It is full of fantastical weather, a thrilling foot, horse, and car chase, a sword fight, and a gunfight. But it is more than just action; it is also full of deep philosophical themes such as order versus chaos, light versus darkness, sanity versus insanity, and transparency versus secrecy. However, this particular essay will focus tightly on the motifs of Creation, Corruption, and Celebration.

By way of a brief introduction to the story, the protagonist, Gabriel Syme, is a poet of order and sanity. His antagonist, Lucian Gregory, is an anarchist poet set on chaos and destruction. Syme intends to stop the anarchists by infiltrating the Central Council of Anarchists. He does so by stealing the vote from Gregory after he convinces the anarchists that Gregory is much too meek and mild to bear the responsibility of Thursday. We soon discover the Council is made up of seven anarchists, each monikered with a day of the week wherein the President of the Council is known as Sunday. From here, the speed of the story picks up in a whirling dervish of chaos, confusion, surprise, and triumph, and ends in celebration and sanity.

Creation

This section will focus on a few selected scenes of the main character Gabriel Syme as he relates to the Creation motif. In Chapter IV, "The Tale of a Detective," we read of Syme's background and how he came to be in the employ of Scotland Yard's newest special corps of policemen, the philosopher detectives. Rather than catching criminals who have committed crimes, these peculiar policemen are trained in philosophy and attend parties and read literature and poetry to anticipate criminal activity and stop it before it occurs.

Syme is recruited and led through a "side-door in the long row of buildings of Scotland Yard."[2] From there, Syme passes one at a time through four

---

[2] Chesterton, *The Man Who Was Thursday.* 84.

intermediate officials, until he enters a room where "the abrupt blackness of which startled him like a blaze of light. It was not the ordinary darkness, in which forms can be faintly traced; it was like going suddenly stone-blind."[3] From out of the darkness, a heavy voice speaks to Syme, "and in some strange way, though there was not the shadow of a shape in the gloom, Syme knew two things: first, that It came from a man of massive stature; and second, that the man had his back to him."[4] Immediately, this unseen man hires Syme into the corps. After some exchange of words between the two, Syme leaves, and we read: "Thus it was that when Gabriel Syme came out again into the crimson light of evening, in his shabby black hat and shabby, lawless cloak, he came out a member of the New Detective Corps for the frustration of the great conspiracy."[5]

For the next two and a half pages, Chesterton bombards the reader with the language of light and darkness, weather, and seasons. Before looking at what Chesterton wrote, perhaps it would be good to

---

[3] Chesterton, The Man Who Was Thursday. 84-85.

[4] Ibid., 85.

[5] Ibid.

remind ourselves of the fourth day of creation as recorded in Genesis 1:14-19:

> Then God said, "Let there be lights in the expanse of the sky to separate the day from the night. They will serve as signs for seasons and for days and years. They will be lights in the expanse of the sky to provide light on the earth." And it was so. God made the two great lights – the greater light to rule over the day and the lesser light to rule over the night – as well as the stars. God placed them in the expanse of the sky to provide light on the earth, to rule the day and the night, and to separate the light from darkness. And God saw that it was good. Evening came and then morning: the fourth day.

The fourth day involves the creation of lights (sun, moon, and stars) as well as a way to mark time (days, years, and seasons). Compare Genesis with the next bit of writing by Chesterton. When Syme first encounters the philosopher detective, Chesterton mentions his unkempt appearance. We are told he was "shabby in those days. He wore an old-fashioned black chimney-pot hat; he was wrapped in a yet more old-fashioned cloak, black and ragged . . . his yellow beard and hair were more unkempt and leonine . . . [and] a long, lean, black cigar . . . stood out from between his tightened teeth, and altogether he looked a very satisfactory specimen of the anarchists upon whom he had vowed a holy war."[6] Compare this with his appearance shortly after being hired by Scotland Yard, while keeping the Genesis passage in mind. After being called out of the void by some invisible voice, Syme trims his beard and hair, he buys a good hat, and he "clad himself in an exquisite summer suit of light blue-grey," from disorder to order, and the mention of a season. [7]

Next, we are transported forward to the story's present-day, where Syme is boarding the steam-tug where he has the "singular sensation of stepping out into something entirely new; not merely into the landscape of a new land, but even into the landscape of a new planet."[8] For the next few paragraphs, Chesterton continues to pile on words and phrases such as: "an entire change in the weather and sky," "naked moon," "naked sky," he calls the moon a "weaker sun," where it "gave, not the sense of bright moonshine, but rather dead daylight," the entire land is "luminous" with an "unnatural

---

[6] Chesterton, The Man Who Was Thursday. 77-78.

[7] Ibid., 85.

[8] Ibid., 86.

discoloration" of some "disastrous twilight," a "sun in eclipse," which made Syme feel as if "he was actually on some other and emptier planet, which circled round some sadder star."[9] Relentlessly, Chesterton continues his description of a "glittering desolation in the moonlit land" where Syme's "chivalric folly glowed in the night like a great fire."[10] Further on, Chesterton writes about the "inhuman landscape," "bright, bleak houses," "a man in the moon," "the clear moon that...lit up Chiswick," and how "day had already begun to break."[11]

Moreover, subtly, this follows the same pattern as Genesis 1:19, which mentions, "Evening came and then morning." The relevant description of Syme during his flashback has him leaving Scotland Yard in the evening. When we arrive in the present, we are in the evening as well, "at about half-past one on a February night."[12] Finally, the scene ends with daylight breaking. Taking in a bigger picture of the entire novel, it follows this same motif, which is not

---

[9] Chesterton, *The Man Who Was Thursday*. 86-87.

[10] Ibid., 87.

[11] Ibid., 87-88.

[12] Ibid., 86.

surprising since the protagonist is Thursday. The opening line of the first chapter reads: "The suburb of Saffron Park lay on the sunset side of London, as red and ragged as a cloud of sunset,"[13] while the novel closes with this final line of the book: "There [Syme] saw the sister of Gregory, the girl with the gold-red hair, cutting lilac before breakfast, with the great unconscious gravity of a girl."[14] The imagery of the fourth day of Creation resounds throughout the story, from start to finish.

Corruption

While corruption typically points to the Fall, Chesterton deals with a specific insidious strain of corruption known intimately by him during his college days attending art school: nihilism. Nihilism is particularly caustic and corrosive as it works its destructive ways both externally and internally. Albert Camus was correct when he opens his *Myth of Sisyphus* with the claim that the only serious philosophical question for a nihilist is suicide.[15] Chesterton brings this idea of Camus into clear focus when he writes about those who merely play at

---

[13] Chesterton, *The Man Who Was Thursday*. 31.

[14] Ibid., 265.

[15] Albert Camus, *The Myth of Sisyphus and Other Essays*, (New York, NY: Vintage International, 1991), 3.

being the anarchists versus those, like Gregory, who claims to be a serious anarchist:

> They are under no illusions; they are too intellectual to think that man upon this earth can ever be quite free of original sin and the struggle. And they mean death. When they say that mankind shall be free at last, they mean that mankind shall commit suicide. When they talk of a paradise without right or wrong, they mean the grave. They have but two objects, to destroy first humanity and then themselves. That is why they throw bombs instead of firing pistols. The innocent rank and file are disappointed because the bomb has not killed the king; but the high-priesthood are happy because it has killed somebody.[16]

The serious anarchist, in the stripe of Gregory, is happy to kill somebody, even if that means themselves.

In this section, we encounter a few short scenes where this attack against being and meaning is present. First, there is the introduction of the story's antagonist, the anarchist poet Lucian Gregory: "His dark red hair parted in the middle was literally like a

---

[16] Chesterton, *The Man Who Was Thursday*. 84.

woman's, and curved into the slow curls of a virgin in a pre-Raphaelite picture. From within this almost saintly oval, however,

> His face projected suddenly broad and brutal, the chin carried forward with a look of cockney contempt. The combination at once tickled and terrified the nerves of a neurotic population. He seemed like a walking blasphemy, a blend of the angel and the ape.[17]

Lucian lacks any sharp distinctions. In one light, he appears male and in another light female. In one setting, an angel and in another an ape, a messenger of light and a brute. It is this amorphous description, this lack of distinction, which marks Lucian's stance against being. At one level, this attack against being is to destroy all external being apart from oneself. Still, the ultimate destruction of being is to extinguish even self and thus to wipe out all being in a single act.

In an early description of Safford Park, we see this language describing the vagueness of the village when we read that "the whole insane village seemed as separate as a drifting cloud."[18] This idea of

---

[17] Chesterton, *The Man Who Was Thursday*. 36.

[18] Ibid., 35.

insanity is a break from reality, and it mistakes the delusion as being real. But the village is not just insane; it has no shape to it at all, no center, no essence, no nature because it is "as separate as a drifting cloud." Drifting clouds do not hold their shape. They lose their distinction as the currents work upon them. They come into being and out of being, and there is nothing to ground them and give them persistence. They take on an appearance of solidity, but in fact, they are anything but solid. This is non-being masking as being.

Later in the story, when Thursday (Syme) and Wednesday (Marquis de Saint Eustache) finish their sword duel, they are running for their lives from the anarchists through a forest. Chesterton draws on his art background here in painting this word scene:

> The inside of the wood was full of shattered sunlight and shaken shadows. They made a sort of shuddering veil, almost recalling the dizziness of a cinematograph. Even the solid figures walking with him Syme could hardly see for the patterns of sun and shade that danced upon them. Now a man's head was lit as with a light of Rembrandt, leaving all else obliterated; now again he had strong and staring white hands with the face of a

negro. The ex-Marquis had pulled the old straw hat over his eyes, and the black shade of the brim cut his face so squarely in two that it seemed to be wearing one of the black half-masks of their pursuers....Was he wearing a mask? Was any one wearing a mask? Was any one anything? This wood of witchery, in which men's faces turned black and white by turns, in which their figures swelled into sunlight and then faded into formless night, this mere chaos of chiaroscuro (after the clear daylight outside), seemed to Syme a perfect symbol of the world in which he had been moving for three days, this world where men took off their beards and their spectacles and their noses, and turned into other people.[19]

Similar to Gregory and the drifting clouds, nothing is as it seems. All is an illusion. There are no real *things*, but vague objects that appear to be one thing and then another thing and then something else entirely. There is no being; all is in flux and, thus, anti-being. "For Gabriel Syme had found in the heart of that sun-splashed wood what many modern painters had found there. He had found the thing which the modern people call Impressionism, which is another name for that final scepticism

---

[19] Chesterton, *The Man Who Was Thursday*. 188-189.

which can find no floor to the universe."[20] This final skepticism is nihilism, where all values and conventions are obliterated, as if by dynamite. Like a drifting cloud, there is no floor; there is no foundation. In an earlier discussion between Lucian and Syme, Lucian says of the anarchist movement, "We hate Rights as we hate Wrongs. We have abolished Right and Wrong."[21] To which Syme responds, "And Right and Left . . ., I hope you abolish them too."[22] Here his request is fulfilled.

Celebration

Finally, the story arrives at a restoration of sorts. Here the madness of non-being gives way to the celebration of being. All things that exist, no matter what they are, are dancing with life. Syme and the other six days dress in attire that does not conceal but instead reveals their true identities.[23] For in wearing his Thursday clothes, Syme "seemed to be for the first time himself and no one else."[24] As the Days of Creation make their way to their seats in the

---

[20] Chesterton, *The Man Who Was Thursday*, 189-190.

[21] Ibid., 54.

[22] Ibid.

[23] Ibid., 253.

[24] Ibid., 254.

garden, they see a "vast carnival of people . . . dancing in motley dress . . . [with] every shape of Nature imitated in some crazy costume. There was a man dressed as a windmill with enormous sails, a man dressed as an elephant, a man dressed as a balloon . . . one dancer dressed like an enormous hornbill, with a beak twice as big as "himself . . . there were a thousand other such objects . . . a dancing lamppost, a dancing apple-tree, a dancing ship."[25] It seemed as if "all the common objects of field and street [were] dancing an eternal jig."[26] The celebration of existence lasted so long that Syme lost track of time. And after all the Days were seated, including Sunday, "that huge masquerade of mankind swayed and stamped in front of them to marching and exultant music. Every couple dancing seemed a separate romance; it might be a fairy dancing "with a pillar-box, or a peasant girl dancing with the moon; but in each case it was, somehow, as absurd as Alice in Wonderland, yet as grace and kind as a love-story."[27] In this final chapter, we have the triumph of life and being with all of Creation dancing with joy in celebration of being alive. What

---

[25] Chesterton, The Man Who Was Thursday. 255.

[26] Ibid.

[27] Ibid., 257-258.

a contrast this is to the anarchist's pessimism that ran throughout the whole of this grand story. In the end, being wins out; existence is celebrated. The fact that anything exists is reason enough to celebrate all of life and all of existence.

Conclusion

The motifs of Creation, Corruption, and Celebration are not unique to this Chesterton work. They show up, sometimes explicitly, sometimes implicitly, in many of his other writings. For Chesterton, Creation appears to be the starting point of *seeing the world as it is*. There is an acknowledgment that we are not the creators of our reality, a message which today's culture needs. There is an external reality that is not dependent upon us; it was here before we arrived and will continue after we are gone. It is not subject to our subjectivity. Sadly, the Corruption of this Creation is seen everywhere. In fact, in his seminal apologetic work *Orthodoxy*, Chesterton reminds us that the only thing provable about Christianity is original sin. The particular failure on display in this novel is brought about by a fatal flaw of thinking in a specific direction. The pessimism of nihilism is corrosive and crushing. Yet, thankfully, it is not the end of the story. Near the end of *The Man Who Was Thursday: A*

Nightmare, order, and sanity are restored during a garden party thrown by Sunday. On display are some of the magnificent works of creation in attendance, full of life and joy, participating in a grand celebration, as if the world were new. After reading this timeless tale of Chesterton's, how will we see the world? Can we celebrate the small and ordinary with the realization that even the small is not so small, where even the ordinary is not so ordinary?

ESCAPING THE MADHOUSE

Clark Weidner

I was panic-stricken upon the discovery that my upper body was constrained by a tight white jacket of sorts. The jacket was covered in buckles which made moving nearly impossible. All I could see around me was white and padded. The room was small; not much bigger than a walk-in closet.

"*Am I in a psych ward?*" I thought. "*There's been a mistake. I shouldn't be here.*"

Just as soon as I had assessed this horrible predicament, in walked a man with a pen and pad in hand, sporting a white lab coat. I felt initially frightened by the sheer size of the man. Standing well over 6 feet in height and as round as he was tall, the moustached giant peered at me through a pair of round spectacles.

"I'm Dr. G." He said. "You aren't well. But I think you still may be able to recover."

"Now wait just a second!" I shouted. "There has been some sort of mix up. I am perfectly fine! I shouldn't be here. I'm no mental patient."

The doctor's face remained unmoved, and he calmly asked, "You really believe there's been a mistake?"

"Yes of course!" I shouted emphatically.

Dr. G. peered over the top of his spectacles and looked sternly into my eyes. "And just why do you think you shouldn't be here?" he asked.

"Because I am sane!" I yelled, angry and frustrated to the point of tears. "I have no idea how I got here! What I do know is that I am intelligent, mild-mannered, normal, and completely capable of functioning in society."

"You sure seem to think so. But how am I supposed to know that? Am I just supposed to take you at your word?" asked the doctor.

I thought, "*What kind of question is that? Can't he see that I am sane?*" But afraid of insulting the large man all I could utter was a simple, "You'll just have to believe me."

"Do you believe in yourself?" asked the doctor.

"Of course I do doctor," I replied. "I just need *you* to believe me."

"Come with me," said Dr. G. "I want to show you something."

"Could you at least take me out of this jacket so I can move my arms?" I asked, feeling quite sorry for myself at this point.

To which he rudely replied, "That remains to be seen."

Dr. G proceeded to lead me out of the padded room and down a long hallway where we passed several doors marked with numbers. Behind each door was a patient; many of which seemed to be much better fitted to the asylum than me.

Take for example, the man I saw wearing feathers strutting around like a chicken on a farm, flapping his arms as if they were actually wings while squawking at us.

I thought, *"Now there's the man that needs this straight jacket."*

Across the hallway from the chicken-man, I saw another patient carving mathematical equations all over the walls. In fact, there was not an inch of the room that wasn't covered in numbers or symbols. He had even inked long complex mathematical theories, numbers, symbols all over his body. He sat in the corner of his cell with a glazed look over his eyes repeating mathematical formulas to himself.

As we continued walking down the hallway, Dr. G pointed out each of the patients he treated in this wing. One claimed to be Jesus Christ. Another claimed unwaveringly to be a famous actor while proceeding to put on the most terrible performance I've ever seen.

But more surprisingly, there was an unusual number of logicians and mathematicians akin to the man who carved all symbols all over the walls. A part of me wondered if some of these men were geniuses who had traded away their sanity for a kind of so-called genius, for the line between the two can be very thin.

Finally, Dr. G stopped at the end of the hallway and looked down over his spectacles at me. He asked, "What do these patients have in common?"

To which I quickly responded, "Well, they are obviously all lunatics."

"How do you know?" asked the doctor.

"Just look at them" I said.

"I look at them every day," replied the doctor, seemingly annoyed. "You said before you are not one of them because you believe that you are sane. *You* clearly believe in yourself. But do you think that they are aware of their *own* insanity?" he asked.

"I suppose they're probably not," I replied.

He continued, "Exactly. They believe that they are completely sane. The actors here believe they are the best actors in the world. The man you saw dressed like a chicken, really believes he *is* a chicken. The mathematician you saw believes that one day he can resolve a completely logical and final explanation for everything we see in the world. These patients believe in themselves."

"And you also believe in yourself. So how do you know you aren't just another patient here?" asked Dr. G.

As I tried to respond, I began struggling to find the words to say. "I um . . . well I, I don't know . . . I suppose I hadn't thought of it that way."

And for the first time I felt the icy chill of self-doubt. How could I prove my sanity to the doctor if he viewed me as just another one of these lunatics? Or worse, could I be a lunatic myself?

Dr. G appeared to read my mind, and in a sympathetic gesture, he said "Let's take off your restraints. You seem harmless enough and there are other rooms I'd like you to see." He removed the straight-jacket and led me to an elevator in which we descended down another floor.

As the elevator opened, I noticed several patients walking through the halls freely. There were no straight jackets on this floor, no locked rooms, no restraints. Rather, the patients on this floor were free to walk about, free to talk with one another, and they were even free to leave had they so chose.

Still, they remained. This baffled me.

"Excuse me . . . Dr. G? . . . Why do they not leave?" I asked. "Don't you worry the patients on this wing could easily escape?"

"They don't *want* to leave," he replied. "The patients on this floor remain here for fear of the outside world. Many of these patients barely leave their room, much less the hospital."

"But don't stare at them!" ordered Dr. G. "If you so much as look at one of these patients for too long you could cause a panic. Many of the patients on this wing fear everything unknown to them. They would read a conspiratorial significance into your every move."

"And why do you suppose they behave this way?" uttered a strange deep voice from behind both myself and Dr. G. I turned to see a man who was also dressed in a lab coat. He introduced himself to me as Mr. Suthers, a local psychiatrist here to perform routine evaluations of the patients.

Mr. Suthers proceeded, "The patients remain here because they are incurable. Their sickness? They act without any rhyme or reason. They may stay here because they fear the unknown, they have no reason for this fear. There is nothing about their actions which one could call sensical. Their causeless actions are why we call them mad."

He continued, "You see regarding sane people, there is a cause for every one of our actions. For example, I chose to speak to you *because* I think Dr. G has misled you, and I felt compelled to correct his mistake. These men are not free to leave here any more than I was free to approach you a moment ago. We don't have free will. But while *our* free will is robbed by reason these patients lost *their* will to insanity."

"You see . . ." continued Mr. Suthers, "every action causes a reaction, and every effect has a prior cause. These men cannot leave because unlike sane men, they have no rhyme or reason for doing *anything*. They likely stay here simply because they've lost the ability to reason. If they could reason at all, they would no doubt have left long ago."

"Wait a second!" I blurted out. I don't know why I interrupted him other than that I genuinely needed clarification. "I thought you said every effect has a prior cause?"

"What's your point?" asked Mr. Suthers.

"My point is that if there is no good reason for these patients to stay here and yet they do . . . have they not broken the chain of causation? If causation can be broken for a madman, can it not be broken for a man?[1] And if we, the sane men, can't break the chain of causation, are you then suggesting that the lunatics on this wing have more free will than I do?"

As I spoke up, I could see the eyebrows of Dr. G lift as he grinned from ear to ear.

"Very well," said Mr. Suthers. "Perhaps lunatics have broken the chain of causation because their actions are void of reason and therefore causeless. If you call that free will, so be it. But what you've called free will, I call insanity."

Dr. G cleared his throat. "May I ask you something Mr. Suthers? How long exactly have you worked with lunatics?"

"Well, for my entire career, sir," replied Mr. Suthers confidently.

"I hope I don't come across as condescending." said Dr. G, "But in my experience, these patients *are* great reasoners. As a matter of fact, all they are good for is reasoning."

"Think about it this way, Mr. Suthers," said Dr. G "There is a grave difference between a healthy man and a lunatic. The healthy man may whistle as he walks; slashing the grass with a stick; kicking his

---

[1] G.K. Chesterton, *Orthodoxy* (New York, NY: Image Books, 2014), 12.

heels, or rubbing his hands. He does these things without care whatsoever. The madman, on the other hand, would think that the lopping of the grass was an attack on private property. He would think that the kicking of the heels was a signal to an accomplice. The madman is not the man who has lost his reason. The madman is the man who has lost everything but his reason."[2]

Mr. Suthers looked perplexed, yet, in some last ditch effort to save face, he declared, "I will not leave this hospital until I have formulated an adequate response to this conundrum. In time, I will have a better explanation for the great illusion of free will. You'll see." And Mr. Suthers headed off towards the other patients.

"I suppose it's time for you to leave," said Dr. G, looking at me in the manner of a proud teacher when his pupil has mastered a subject.

"Really?" I asked. But then I thought, "Where will I go? How do you leave a place if you don't know how you got there?"

I looked around the room for an exit, but when I turned to ask Dr. G for directions, he was a great distance off, whistling and rubbing his hands as he walked away.

---

[2] Chesterton, *Orthodoxy*, 13.

Just as suddenly as he had appeared in my cell. He was gone from my side.

There were, however, two double doors ahead of me. Above the doors hung a red and white exit sign. After breathing a sigh of relief, I began racing toward the exit.

When I opened the doors, I was shocked. The doors appeared to lead directly out of the hospital and into a moonlit night sky. But I wasn't outside. I was still in a room, for I could see the perimeter of walls surrounding me.

I also noticed that I stood in a garden of sorts. There were colorful floral arrangements which would make for a stunning view except they all appeared to be artificial. The garden didn't have the smell one would expect of fresh flowers, nor was there any warm sunlight.

Looking above in curiosity I saw a model of the entire cosmos. There were stars, planets, and galaxies which looked much smaller than I had imagined.

Because of the small size of the planets, I began to wonder if this was a museum or an art class for patients; the whole thing was eerie. While it seemed odd that a museum would be connected to a madhouse, I had begun to assume anything was possible after all I'd seen. The galaxies above me were just plastic models of the universe. I could reach out and touch every one of them.

"Excuse me, sir. You're standing on my flowers. Can I help you?" said a voice over my shoulder.

"Oh I am sorry." I looked down to discover I had crushed about a half a dozen artificial daisies while looking at the plastic cosmos above. "I'm lost. I was just er . . . discharged from the hospital, and I thought I had found the exit. It appears I'm mistaken."

"No, no, no! You aren't mistaken. My name is Mr. McCabe. I am the keeper of the grounds here. You're no longer in the hospital. But you can always go back inside if you're lost."

"Okay. So how do I leave this museum, or garden, or wait, where am I?" I asked.

"This is no museum or garden," replied Mccabe. "This is the universe," he said as he went back to watering his artificial plants.

Suddenly I feared I'd wandered into another patient's room. This time Dr. G wasn't around to breathe some sanity into the situation.

I began to notice small trees throughout the garden as well. But they had no roots, so it seemed to me they could easily fall over.

"Mr. McCabe," I said, accidentally bumping into a plastic tree as it tipped over behind me, "Suppose I want to leave this "universe" of yours . . . "

"Impossible!" interrupted Mccabe. "For how could you leave everything that *is*. There is nothing beyond what you can see here."

"Well then, how did you get here?" I asked.

"What do you mean?" questioned Mccabe who now seemed to be suspicious of me.

"I mean if this is all there is . . . were you always here? Where did you come from?"

"It's simple," said Mccabe. "A series of events brought me here. Events out of my control or one could say a complete accident . . . Have you not met my friend Mr. Suthers? I'm sure he could tell you how causation works."

"Yes, but the planets above you are just plastic models. There is a real world outside of this small room." As soon as I said this I remembered something Mr. G had said about lunatics being great reasoners. To change McCabe's mind would be more like casting out a devil than arguing with a philosopher.[3]

"And how do you know that?" asked McCabe. "You don't even know how *you* got here much less,

---

[3] Chesterton, *Orthodoxy*. 16.

how you can leave. I suppose you also believe in magic or elves and fairies," said McCabe mockingly.

For good reason, I didn't deny this accusation. I thought McCabe maybe a bit deranged when it comes to what's real or not.

McCabe rolled his eyes as I blankly stared back at him. "Well then, so be it. I'll leave you to your absurd imagination."

As he walked away the word "imagination" lingered with me. Imagination. I looked up at the plastic cosmos above and thought of a plan.

Somehow I managed to ascend one of the plastic trees. Of course, I had to do my best to balance as it began to wobble beneath me.

I began pressing against the model of the plastic cosmos and to my delight a ceiling tile opened above me.

Pulling myself upwards, I could see a light above me, leaving the artificial and harsh light of the white-washed asylum walls. I could feel the warm breeze blowing on my back as the sun touched my skin. Before long, I stood on top of the roof. Looking across from the hospital, I noticed a sign that read Hanwell Lunatic Asylum.

Relieved to be free, I closed my eyes and breathed in the fresh air. But suddenly I heard a loud ringing.

Someone's phone was ringing loudly in the once quiet library to which I had come to study for a philosophy exam.

Startled and relieved that I had only been dreaming I thought, "I'm awake. Thank God I'm awake."

Suddenly I had lost interest in further studying *A Treatise on Human Nature*. Instead I elected to crack open another book; one that would keep me from falling asleep again: *Phantastes*.

As I opened this classic fairy tale, I was reminded again of how it felt to walk out of a padded room and have the straight-jacket removed.

THE FREEDOM OF BOUNDARIES

Zak Schmoll

G.K. Chesterton cherished human freedom; however, he did not believe that freedom ought to be exercised to fulfill all human desires. Rather, a man should willingly submit to moral law, established by God for the benefit of humanity, as a way to experience the true freedom that God intended. A lover of paradox, it is evident that Chesterton's perspective on human freedom could be understood as a contradiction by some. If Man is truly free, then he should not have to subject himself to moral law. Conversely, if Man is not subject to moral law, then Chesterton argues he is not truly free. The key to unraveling this seeming contradiction rests in the fact that the truest expression of freedom can only be found when one is rightly aligned with God's law. When that dynamic is out of alignment, any freedom that man might believe he has is nothing but an illusion.

By modern standards, Chesterton took a rather curious position on boundaries. While most people contend that boundaries are the imposition of a higher power impinging on the freedom of those subjected to the rule of that power, Chesterton realized that boundaries can be beneficial and actually useful in preserving freedom itself. He explains, "We might fancy some children playing on the flat grassy top of some tall island in the sea. So long as there was a wall round the cliff's edge they could fling themselves into every frantic game and make the place the noisiest of nurseries."[1] There was no danger on top of the mountain because of the boundary. While some may have considered the wall to be a restriction of the children's freedom, it is worth considering how many things the children were able to do because they did not have to fear. Tossing a football would not be accompanied by the fear that the receiver would go tumbling into the ocean. Their environment would not ruin their game. The freedom to truly enjoy what was meant for them to enjoy was only possible because they were protected from the danger that surrounded them. Chesterton went on to describe a world

---

[1] G.K. Chesterton, *Orthodoxy* (Chicago: Moody Publishers, 2009), 216.

without boundaries by saying, "But the walls were knocked down, leaving the naked peril of the precipice. They did not fall over; but when their friends returned to them they were all huddled in terror in the center of the island; and their song had ceased."[2] The children understood the situation they were in. Because they did not want to fall off the edge, recognizing that a fall was the worst possible outcome, they sat in the middle of the island. No motion was better than potential danger.

The irony of the entire situation is that removing the boundary had absolutely no impact on the degree of freedom that these children had. The patch of grass had not changed in size whatsoever. The children still could take just as many steps safely as they could before. However, without the wall, the element of fear crept into their minds. They did not want to get too close to the edge because there was no longer a wall that would hold them in safely. Without the boundary, there was no guarantee that everything would be all right. Instead, exercising their freedom fully meant taking a risk that a strong wind might blow and have fatal consequences if they got too close to the edge.

---

[2] Chesterton, *Orthodoxy*. 216.

Because of this risk, the children then voluntarily restricted their freedom to an even greater degree than the wall ever did. In fact, as it turned out, the wall itself was never even a restriction. There was no land outside of the wall. They were on a plateau. What might seem to be a restriction of freedom and a boundary actually turned out to be what allowed these children to enjoy the entire plot of land they were given to enjoy.

Chesterton wanted to encourage humanity to enjoy all the good things in life. He wrote, "A man cannot expect any adventures in the land of anarchy. But a man can expect any number of adventures if he goes traveling in the land of authority."[3] Chesterton believed that most ordinary people desire a, "combination of something that is strange with something that is secure."[4] In his typically witty fashion, he quipped, "What could be more glorious than to brace one's self up to discover New South Wales and then realize, with a gush of happy tears, that it was really old South Wales."[5] This combination of adventure and security is why man desires boundaries. It is wonderful to have the

---

[3] Chesterton, *Orthodoxy*. 234.

[4] Ibid., 21.

[5] Ibid., 20

freedom to go to Australia, but there is something extraordinarily comforting about being home again in the United Kingdom.

To transition this argument into moral terms, it is wonderful to have the ability to do anything, but there is naturally danger associated with certain activities. Surely a man is free to put his hand in a fire, but he is not free of the painful consequences of doing so. Therefore, it is reasonable to self-impose a boundary in this situation. An individual makes a conscious decision based on some external authority, in this case, experience, to not participate in a specific activity. Certainly, it is a restriction of freedom, but it is voluntarily coming under the direction of a set of guidelines that provide an ultimate benefit. In this case, subscribing to a belief system that advises one not to put his hand into the fire will lead directly to an avoidance of pain, an objectively good outcome based on the worldview of this person has embraced.

Chesterton highlighted the importance of boundaries as necessary for protecting freedom because he held a person's philosophy as a matter of high regard. The shape and condition of those boundaries would be defined by the philosophy of the person or deity who put them there. Chesterton pointed out the absurdity of a man who espoused a philosophy claiming that life did not matter.

> At any innocent tea-table we may easily hear a man say, 'Life is not worth living.' We regard it as we regard the statement that it is a fine day; nobody thinks that it can possibly have any serious effect on the man or on the world. And yet if that utterance were really believed, the world would stand on its head.[6]

It is not hard to conclude that the shape of the boundaries that encircle a world where life is not worth living would be substantially different than the boundaries that surround a world where life is worth living.

In the first world, murder and suicide might be more honorable and noble than birthdays. In the first world, reckless endangerment might actually be celebrated as a way to help those who are stuck in this pointless life find their way out of it. If humanity consistently embraced the philosophy that life was not worth living, there would be no one left on earth because all would have terminated their meaningless lives. The picture of a universe

---

[6] G. K. Chesterton, *Heretics* (New York: John Lane Company, 1919), 2.

where life is worth living is incredibly different than the picture of a universe where life is not worth living.

Therefore, philosophy is naturally of chief importance. As Chesterton said, "We think that for a general about to fight an enemy, it is important to know the enemy's numbers, but still more important to know the enemy's philosophy."[7] In order to win the battle, it is vital for the general to understand his enemy's philosophy and tactics. Numbers matter, but they are not the chief concern. A terrible general can easily squander superior numbers, and an excellent general can triumph with fewer troops. The philosophy makes all the difference, and it defines the success that the army is going to have. Similarly, the boundaries that a society sets based on the philosophy that it embraces can make all of the difference between successful manifestations of freedom or utter destruction and chaos.

Freedom, therefore, needs to be understood in the context of the framework that surrounds it. These boundaries can also be positive or negative according to Chesterton.

---

[7] Chesterton, *Heretics.* 3.

> A young man may keep himself from vice
> by continually thinking of disease. He
> may keep himself from it also by
> continually thinking of the Virgin Mary.
> There may be question about which
> method is the more reasonable, or even
> about which is the more efficient. But
> surely there can be no question about
> which is the more wholesome.[8]

In one situation, the young man is faced with potential danger, but in the other he is viewing that which is actually good. There is a difference between avoiding evil and embracing good. This is again a question of philosophy. For Chesterton, these are not equivalent by any means, and it is much better to establish boundaries that encourage the good. Thinking back to the children playing on the plateau, the purpose of the boundary was not to prevent them from falling or even restrict their freedom but rather to encourage them to play all over the plateau. Yes, it had the associated benefit of keeping the children safe, but the proper purpose of the boundary was to encourage good behavior.

The chief problem in Chesterton's day should sound familiar to contemporary readers. In determining the shape of these boundaries that are

---

[8] Chesterton, *Heretics.* 8.

meant to encourage freedom to do good, inevitably, the moral relativist will chime in and challenge whether or not that which is good can actually be discerned from that which is bad. Chesterton saw the mental gymnastics people were willing to go through in his day and lamented, "The modern man says, 'Let us leave all these arbitrary standards and embrace liberty.' This is, logically rendered, 'Let us not decide what is good, but let it be considered good not to decide it.'"[9] It is difficult to determine that which is good, and it is a controversial exercise to say the least because of the modern infatuation with either moral relativism or simultaneously affirming worldviews with different, objective claims. Therefore, it is tempting to leave this question for another day. It is tempting to try to avoid the conversation of actually discovering what is right or wrong in the world.

The problem, of course, with this approach is that it is impossible to establish the necessary boundaries before deciding what shape they need to be in. As Chesterton wrote, "Nobody has any business to use the word 'progress' unless he has a definite creed and a cast-iron code of morals."[10]

---

[9] Chesterton, *Heretics*, 10.

[10] Ibid.,11.

There is no way to move ahead with establishing these boundaries or make any progress without first settling the question of what is actually right and wrong. However, without these boundaries, it is impossible to truly exercise freedom, so the challenge of civilization is to first understand morality so that the foundation can be established. Without the foundation, the entire exercise in and of itself is going to collapse from within. Freedom, therefore, cannot be exercised properly without boundaries, and boundaries are not able to be determined without first deciding where they should be put up.

In determining where these boundaries ought to be built, Chesterton came to believe that Christianity provided the best framework for explaining the world and the way that it was. One of the chief attractions that drew him to Christianity was the fact that it allowed for freedom. He cherished the ability for people to exercise their free will, and he understood that the entire process of true freedom could only be recognized within the context of a Christian worldview. "The more I considered Christianity, the more I found that while it had established a rule and order, the chief aim of that order was to give room for good things to run wild."[11]

Again, some may contend that this is a restriction of freedom. Because Christianity had established rules and order, absolute freedom was indeed constrained. However, it was constrained by the individual. It was brought upon himself through his own decision to subscribe to the teachings of the Christian religion. Chesterton compared one who was upset about the boundaries of Christianity to one who ultimately shuts himself out of any world because he has rebelled against the world itself. "It is all the difference between being free from them, as a man is free from a prison, and being free of them as a man is free of a city."[12] Christianity allows man to be free from boundaries, but that does not mean that he is free of them. No boundary is imposed on the Christian, but God imposes boundaries that define what is best for human flourishing and what exercises of freedom are most consistent with that purpose. People freely choose to subscribe to those boundaries by virtue of being Christians. Therefore, it comes down to a theological question for

---

[11] Chesterton, *Orthodoxy*, 144.

[12] Ibid., 145.

Chesterton. He was chiefly concerned with what religion provided the best environment for good things to run wild. Based on the boundaries that outlined the best possible use of human freedom and encouraged that behavior, he came to the conclusion that Christianity was the best candidate to determine where those boundaries ought to be established.

The right answer was determined, again, based on philosophy. "The religions of the earth do *not* greatly differ in rites and forms; they do greatly differ in what they teach."[13] What made the difference was ultimately the person of Jesus Christ. It was the teaching and the doctrine that made the difference. He explained, "If the divinity is true it is certainly terribly revolutionary. That a good man may have his back to the wall is no more than we knew already; but that God could have his back to the wall is a boast for all insurgents for ever."[14] Because of this commitment to courage and the uniqueness of Christianity, Chesterton found that it was, "the most adventurous and manly of all theologies."[15] In this way, it fit perfectly with

---

[13] Chesterton, *Orthodoxy*, 193.

[14] Ibid., 206.

[15] Ibid., 207.

Chesterton's original assertion that ordinary people desire adventure and are pleasantly surprised when they are able to avoid the discomfort in that adventure. Being what he considered an ordinary man himself, it should be no surprise to anyone that he was drawn to Christianity. If adventure is what people desire, then a theology with a God who was "a rebel as well as a king" seemed to be one that was worth following.[16]

The fulfillment of those desires then completes Chesterton's causal chain that leads to his affirmation of the proper type and use of human freedom. He wrote, "Christianity satisfies suddenly and perfectly man's ancestral instinct for being the right way up; satisfies it supremely in this; that by its creed joy becomes something gigantic and sadness something special and small."[17] There is a simple and straightforward joy that overcomes a man when he finds a philosophy that is consistent with reality. That is what Chesterton found in Christianity. He understood that he wanted the world to be the right way, and as he understood Christianity more and more, his instincts about desiring the good were reconfirmed by what

---

[16] Chesterton, *Orthodoxy,* 206.

[17] Ibid., 238.

Christianity taught. He found the shape that he ought to build these boundaries in.

CHESTERTON AT THE MOVIES

Seth Myers

I have a story that will make you
believe in God[1]

– Yann Martel, Life of Pi

Comparative religion is very comparative
indeed... it is only comparatively successful
when it tries to compare. When we come to
look at it closely we find we are really trying
to compare things that are really quite
incomparable.[2]

-- GK Chesterton, The Everlasting Man

---

[1] Yann Martel, *Life of Pi* (New York:L Harcourt, 2001). x.

[2] G.K. Chesterton, *The Everlasting Man* (Mansfield Centre: Martino, 2014), 78.

I don't mean to water down my Christianity into a vague kind of universalism with Buddha and Mohammed all being more or less equal to Jesus – not at all! But neither do I want to tell God (or my friends) where he can and cannot be seen.[3]

– Madeleine L'Engle, Walking on Water

Introduction: The Melting Pot of Culture and Faith

What would G.K. Chesterton think of our increasingly multicultural world? How might he respond when it shows up in so many books and films? Pondering the question brings to mind the wisdom that new issues are often old issues in modern dress; it also brings to mind Chesterton's masterpiece on the course of history, *The Everlasting Man*, which influenced C.S. Lewis in his journey to the Christian faith. Lewis said of it:

Then I read Chesterton's *Everlasting Man* and for the first time saw the whole Christian outline of history set out in a form that seemed to me to make sense . . . You will remember that I already thought

---

[3] Madeleine L'Engel, *Walking on Water: Reflections on Faith and Art* (Colorado Springs: Waterbrook, 2001), 28.

Chesterton the most sensible man alive 'apart from his Christianity.'[4]

Our world grows smaller as the West, East, Middle East and global South intermingle on a daily basis. Traditions that have been inextricably linked with age-old religions jostle with each other, and their adherents must dialogue with each other, not just in terms of culture, but also regarding philosophy and religion. Despite projections of the death of religion from Voltaire, Friedrich Nietzsche, and John Lennon, sociologist Peter Berger states, "The world today is massively religious, is anything but the secularized world that had been predicted (whether joyfully or despondently) by so many analysts of modernity."[5] In fact the word *culture* admits its basis in religion, as the root *cultus* (from which *cult* is derived) references divine worship. In *Leisure: The Basis for Culture*, Joseph Pieper shows how such *cultus* implies that a culture makes space to contemplate meaning beyond the daily, utilitarian world of work and even of science.[6] Hence, *multiculturalism* includes not just the study

---

[4] C.S. Lewis, *Surprised by Joy* (Glasgow: Collins, 1955), 178.

[5] Quoted in Daniel A. Seidell, *God in the Gallery:A Christian Embrace of Modern Art* (Grand Rapids: Baker Academic, 2008), 47.

[6] Josef Pieper, *Leisure: The Basis of Culture* (San Francisco: Ignatius Press, 2009), 15.

of culture but also the religious practices on which cultures are founded. Nearly one hundred years ago, Chesterton examined the cultures and religions that define today's world in *The Everlasting Man.* He includes the thought (both religious and philosophical) behind Asian culture (Confucianism, Buddhism, and Hinduism), the Middle East (Islam) and the Christian faith which has contended with cultures both East and West.

Chesterton thus has a great deal to say about the multicultural thrust of such recent films as Yann Martel's religiously syncretistic *Life of Pi* and Madeleine L' Engle's *Wrinkle in Time* which draws from the wisdom of many cultures and religions. Since Chesterton finishes *The Everlasting Man* by considering Christmas, with some sense of fun and good cheer, we will consider how he might view popular holiday-fare productions such as *Hallmark* Christmas romances and the recently released *Last Christmas.*

The easiest way for Hollywood to come to grips with the situation is to give all faiths an equal seat at the table, an admittedly necessary step for civil discussion. The risk of religious multiculturalism, however, is that considering all faiths to be true in fact violates the unique claims of each religion. As Ravi Zacharias states:

All religions are not the same. All religions do not point to God. All religions do not say that all religions are the same. At the heart of every religion is an uncompromising commitment to a particular way of defining who God is or is not and accordingly, of defining life's purpose . . . Every religion at its core is exclusive.[7]

Consequently Zacharias often points out that it is not the case that religions look different but are at heart the same, but the reverse: they may look similar, but, at heart, each makes unique and contradictory claims about reality.

Respect for the various faith traditions is important. Lesslie Newbigin, Christian missionary to India for forty years, warned that "there is something deeply repulsive in the attitude, sometimes found among Christians, which makes only grudging acknowledgement of the faith, the godliness and the nobility to be found in the lives of non-Christians."[8] Nevertheless, at the level of claims to truth, one is compelled to augment Piotr Mlodozeniec's well-meaning "Coexist" image turned

---

[7] Ravi Zacharias, *Jesus Among Other Gods* (Nashville: Word Publishing, 2000), 7.

[8] Lesslie Newbigin, *The Gospel in a Pluralist Society* (Grand Rapids, Mich.: Eerdmans, 1989), 180.

popular bumper sticker (where the Islamic Crescent, Star of David and Christian Cross constitute the "C," "X" and "T" respectively) with another bumper sticker "Contradict: They can't all be true" (in which Daoist yin-yang, Egyptian and tribal religious symbols among others augment the Star of David, Crescent and Cross).[9] Commitment to a single stance on an issue was classic Chesterton, who declared, "Merely having an open mind is nothing. The object of opening the mind, as of opening the mouth, is to shut it again on something solid."[10] The principle holds for evaluating religious systems, as Chesterton states

> Comparative religion is very comparative indeed . . . it is only comparatively successful when it tries to compare. When we come to look at it closely we find we are really trying to compare things that are really quite incomparable.[11]

---

[9] Frank Turek, "Cross Examined," accessed November 22, 2019, www.crossexamined.org.

10 G. K. Chesterton, Autobiography, Project Gutenberg Australia, accessed November 27, 2019, http://gutenberg.net.au/ebooks13/1301201h.html.

[11] G.K. Chesterton, *The Everlasting Man* (Mansfield Centre: Martino Publishing, 2014), 78.

Chesterton and the Many Flavors of Pi

Chesterton and Hollywood have some differences to iron out on the matter of comparing religions. *The Life of Pi* provides the clearest example of the tension between respecting and believing competing religions, as the young Pi Patel adopts Hinduism, Christianity and Islam simultaneously (which works until the Hindu pandit, Muslim imam and Christian priest simultaneously converge on Pi and his family at the seashore). The Patels properly object: "They're separate religions! They have nothing common" (then playfully taunting with "so, Swami Jesus, will you go on hajj this year?"). [12] But Pi finds something beautiful, if not ineffable, in each tradition. Of his first faith, Hinduism, he says:

> I feel at home in a Hindu temple. I am aware of Presence, not personal the way we usually feel presence, but something larger. My heart still skips a beat when when I catch sight of the murti, of God Residing, in the inner sanctum of a temple. Truly I am in a sacred womb, a place where everything is born, and it is my sweet luck to behold its living core.[13]

---

[12] Yann Martel, *Life of Pi* (New York: Harcourt, 2001), 70-72.

[13] Ibid., 48.

Pi next meets Jesus Christ in a church nestled amidst some small hills of Munnar, Tamil Nadu:

> There was a painting. Was this the murti? Something about a human sacrifice. An angry god who had to be appeased with blood . . . [Father Martin] told me a story . . . and what a story. The first thing that drew me in was disbelief. What? Humanity sins but it's God's Son who pays the price . . . what a downright weird story. What peculiar psychology. I asked for another story . . . [but] their religion had one Story . . . it was story enough for them. That a god should put up with adversity, I could understand . . . But humiliation? Death? I couldn't imagine Lord Krishna consenting to be stripped naked, whipped, mocked, dragged through the streets and, to top it off, crucified.[14]

Islam followed right behind, hardly a year later:

> He was a Sufi, a Muslim mystic. He sought fana, union with God, and his relationship with God was personal and loving. 'If you take two steps towards God,' he used to tell me, 'God runs to you.' . . . I challenge anyone to understand Islam, its spirit, and not to love it. It is a beautiful religion of

---

[14] Martel, *Life of Pi*, 54.

brotherhood and devotion . . . we prayed
together and we practiced the ninety-nine
revealed names of God. He was a hafiz, one
who knows the Qur'an by heart, and he
sang it in a slow, simple chant. My Arabic
was never very good, but I loved its sound.
The guttural eruptions and long flowing
vowels rolled just beneath my
comprehension like a beautiful brook.[15]

Pi also describes ecstatic moments when he felt
God's presence in nature, concluding "the presence
of God is the finest of rewards."[16]

Pi even sees atheists as brothers in faith, at least
compared to agnostics: "like me, they go as far as the
legs of reason will carry them – and then they
leap."[17] Yet, he still opposes their atheism. To the
claims of his biology teacher, Mr. Kumar, that
"religion is darkness," Pi declares religion is
anything but darkness, and when Mr. Kumar
explains that it was science and medicine, not God,
that saved him from his polio, Pi reasons "what a
terrible disease that must be if it could kill God in a
man."[18] But it is doubt, like Chesterton's open jaws

---

[15] Martel, *Life of Pi*, 62-63.

[16] Ibid., 63.

[17] Ibid., 28.

[18] Ibid., 48.

of indecision that bothers Pi: even Christ anguished in doubt in Gethsemane, "but we must move one" Pi responds, "to choose doubt as a way of life is akin to choosing immobility as a means of transportation."[19]

Chesterton, however, cannot follow Pi in collecting religions like trading cards. He thus rejects:

> The phrase of facile liberality uttered again and again . . . [that] 'the religions of the earth do not differ greatly in rites and forms; but they are the same in what they teach.' It is false; it is the opposite of the fact . . . they agree in the mode of teaching; what they differ about is the thing to be taught.[20]

Chesterton sifts world religions into two bins: Christianity and Buddhism. C. S. Lewis followed Chesterton in this when wrestling with his own beliefs, declaring that Christianity and Hinduism "were really the only two answers possible . . . everything else was either a preparation for, or else (in the French sense) a vulgarisation of these . . .

---

[19] Martel, *Life of Pi*, 48.

[20] G.K. Chesterton, *Orthodoxy* (www.digireads.com), 96.

(*Everlasting Man* was helping me here)." [21] [22] Thus, Christianity followed Judaism, with Islam building on both, while Gautama Buddha sprouted Buddhism from the seed of Hinduism, with other Eastern philosophies and religions following or related. But Chesterton claimed that even Christianity and Buddhism were highly dissimilar, despite claims to the contrary. Resemblances are only superficial, for instance their moral codes and compassion. Such resemblances are common to humanity, not only to specific religions. Buddhists and Christians alike disapprove of cruelty and excess:

> But to say that Buddhism and Christianity give the same account of these things is simply false. All humanity does agree that we are in a net of sin. Most of humanity agrees that there is some way out. But as to what is the way out, I do not think that there are two institutions in the universe which contradict each other so flatly as Buddhism and Christianity.[23]

---

[21] Lewis first came to admit that "God is God" and thus became a Theist but it took up to two years for him to decide on the Christian faith, though Alister McGrath argues it took just one, from Spring, 1930 to Autumn, 1931. See C.S. Lewis, Surprised by Joy (1955) and Alister McGrath, C.S. Lewis – A Life (Tyndale, 2013).

[22] C.S. Lewis, *Surprised by Joy* (Glasgow: Collins, 1955), 188.

[23] Chesterton, *Orthodoxy*, 97.

Chesterton's *Orthodoxy*: Christ and the Buddha

The artwork of the two religions, Chesterton claims, provides the clue to their radical difference: "the Buddhist saint always has his eyes shut, while the Christian saint always has them very wide open . . . the Buddhist is looking with a certain intentness inwards. The Christian is staring with a frantic intentness outwards."[24] As a pantheist, the Buddhist finds reality within himself, while the Christian finds himself separated from God and searching for reconciliation. This fundamental metaphysical difference has significant consequences. Worship and even love are affected: for the Buddhist, everything is part of a monolithic reality, and the worship of such an all-consuming world soul amounts to loving it "only in order that man may throw himself into it;" it is a "monotonous courtship" with oneself. [25] [26] The Christian, by

---

[24] Chesterton, *Orthodoxy*, 98.

[25] I am here reminded of the story of the Buddhist ordering a hot dog, and when asked what he would like on it, answers "make me one with everything." I credit my philosophy major brother for that insight.

[26] Ibid., 98.

contrast, is "glad that God has broken the universe into little pieces, because they are living pieces:" "love desires personality; therefore love desires division," it is a case of saying "'little children, love one another' rather than to tell one large person to love himself."[27]

Such pantheism as Buddhism is morally challenged by virtue of its structure, Chesterton further claims. "Pantheism implies in its nature that one thing is as good as another; whereas action implies in its nature that one thing is greatly preferred to another."[28]   A sense of passivity is attached to pantheism, as the shuttered eyes of the Buddha contemplate the unreality of existence. Chesterton thus connects metaphysics with ethics:

> By insisting specially on the immanence of God we get introspection, self-isolation, quietism, social indifference – Tibet. By insisting on the transcendence of God we get wonder, curiosity, moral and political adventure, righteous indignation – Christendom. By insisting that God is inside man, man is always inside himself.

---

[27] Chesterton, *Orthodoxy*, 98.

[28] Ibid., 99.

By insisting that God transcends man, man has transcended himself.[29]

Further, the suffering Christ, admired by Pi, is the epitome of such a heroic moral crusade, thereby actually *enhancing* his divinity. Chesterton continues:

> That a good man could have his back to the wall is no more than we knew already; but that God could have his back to the wall is a boast for all insurgents for ever. Christianity is the only religion on earth that has felt that omnipotence made God incomplete. Christianity alone has felt that of all creeds, Christianity has added courage to the virtues of the Creator. For the only courage worth calling courage must necessarily mean that the soul passes a breaking point – and does not break.[30]

Pi the Hindu

We now turn back to Pi, who can hardly breathe without his faith, confessing that "a germ of religious exaltation, no bigger than a mustard seed, was sown in me and left to germinate. It has never stopped growing . . . [though] many people seem to

---

[29] Chesterton, *Orthodoxy*, 100.

[30] Ibid., 103.

lose God along life's way [but] that was not my case."[31] But Pi is first and ultimately a Hindu, with his belief in Brahman nirguna (without qualities, beyond understanding, beyond description), Brahman saguna (with a multitude of names and qualities, Krishna the loving, Shiva the righteous, Shakti the powerful, Ganesha the wise), as well as Brahman expressed in all living things, including in ourselves (atman). The spiritual force inside us, the Atman, is the same force as the infinite Brahman, Pi claims, explaining that "the individual soul touches upon the world like a well reaches for the water table,"[32] drawing on the Bank of Karma, the fruits of our deeds, to fund its journey of liberation from self and reunion with Brahman. Brahman is not to be possessed, however, just as Krishna vanishes the moment the milkmaids with whom he dances in the forest seek his embrace: "so it is that we should not be jealous with God."[33] God, however, can be jealous, and powerful in his own way, as Pi cites various stories of gods incarnated as avatars battling evil "with shine and power and might."[34] But they thus

---

[31] Chesterton, *Orthodoxy*, 47.

[32] Ibid., 48.

[33] Ibid., 49.

[34] Ibid., 55.

only make the humility and suffering of Jesus more perplexing, even though Jesus does such things as declare a fig tree to be eternally fruitless for its lack of forethought to provide him shade. Pi might do well to consider Chesterton's point that Jesus's suffering and humility exemplify his courage, inspiring as both king and rebel.

Pi thus says of Jesus "I could not get Him out of my head. I still can't."[35] Part of Pi's problem with Christ is the commitment he requires:

> To "to one born in a religion where the battle for a single soul can be a relay race run over many centuries . . . the quick resolution of Christianity has a dizzying effect. If Hinduism flows placidly like the Ganges, then Christianity bustles like Toronto at rush hour . . . in a moment you are lost or saved.[36]

But Pi's criteria for God suit Christ as well as the rest, his list including elation, joy, a moral rather than intellectual sense of the universe, and the foundations of love, presence and ultimate purpose.[37]

---

[35] Chesterton, *Orthodoxy*, 56.

[36] Ibid., 57.

[37] Ibid., 58.

Martel claims the meaning of *Life of Pi* centers about love and the presence of God, which can describe Dante's *Divine Comedy* as well. In two short but critical chapters, Martel speaks of joy, a moral sense more important than an intellectual understanding of things, and love. Of God's apparent silence, Martel can offer only the comforting thought of:

> *"An intellect confounded yet a trusting sense of presence and of ultimate purpose."*[38]

Dante answers Martel's longing for *love*, divine *presence* and *purpose* in the famous final lines of *Paradise*:

> Already were all my will and my desires
>
> Turned – as a wheel in equal balance – by
>
> The Love that moves the sun and the other stars.[39]

The *Love* (God) that "moves" our will and desires endows us with *purpose*, ordering the ways of our

---

[38] Martel, *Life of Pi*, 63.

[39] Date Alighieri, *Paradise* tr. Anthony Esolen (New York: Modern Library, 2007), Canto 33, l. 143-145.

heart. As to presence, the wheel that turns not just ourselves but the "sun and other stars" *is* the *presence* of God, divine Love; it evokes not just the wheel of fate spun by Lady Fortune, Boethius's guide eight centuries prior, in which we travel from the periphery of an often cruel fate to the comforting presence of God at the center, but the notion of Medieval Christian mystic Nicholas of Cusa a century and a half after Dante, in which God is considered as both center and circumference of the world. [40] [41] We will soon see how differently the Asian philosophies and religions conceive of a wheel.

Everlasting Man's Own Wrinkles in Time

Chesterton further scrutinizes the history of religions, East and West, Christian and Pagan, Ancient and Modern in *The Everlasting Man*; a brief look at its key themes can better help us untangle the devout but eclectic Pi from his web of contradictory faiths. It can also enlighten us on the patchwork of thinkers, religious, philosophical, literary, scientific

---

[40] Boethius, *The Consolation of Philosophy* (Oxford: Oxford University PRess, 2000).

[41] As discussed in C.S. Lewis, *The Discarded Image: An Introduction to Medieval and Renaissance Literature* (Cambridge: Cambridge University Press, 1994), 87.

and otherwise, found in Madeleine L'Engle's *Wrinkle in Time*. L'Engle's erudition is undeniable, citing and quoting figures from Horace to Seneca to Dante to Shakespeare to Gandhi. Her Christian faith, however, appears muddled when she cites Scripture and Saint Francis along with figures such as Buddha. Yet, her reliance on Christian scripture in her writing betrays the image of eclectic religious faith. When listing Earth's fighters in the cosmic battle against evil, Mrs Who first cites Jesus's "the light shineth in darkness" before her list of artists, scientists, and religious figures of various traditions. While being transported towards battle with the IT, the group rests in some breathtaking landscape and Mrs. Whatsit calls attention to a resonating voice arising and reading from Psalms, "Sing unto the Lord a new song, and his praise from the end of the earth . . . let them give glory unto the Lord!"[42] [43] Through such references and her citations of figures from across the disciplinary and religious spectrum, L'Engle seems to be proving the point that "There is nothing so secular that it cannot

---

[42] Lewis, *The Discarded Image*, 85.

[43] Ibid., 64.

be sacred, and that is one of the deepest messages of the Incarnation."[44]

Chesterton helps us unravel Pi as he in fact claims to reverse the preference of the shipping official, and of God, for the story version with the animals: "It is exactly when we do regard man as an animal that we know he is not an animal."[45] Considering the most primal form of man imaginable, the caveman, Chesterton turns once again to art to illustrate his point. We may find pictures of reindeer on cave walls drawn by cavemen, but have never found a picture of a man drawn by a reindeer. "Art is the signature of man."[46] Neither might a bird have ever "carefully selected forked twigs and pointed leaves to express the piercing piety of the Gothic, but turned to broad foliage and black mud when he sought in a darker mood to call up the heavy columns of Bel and Ashtaroth."[47] Religion did not evolve from devotion paid to natural objects but the need to worship existed first; hieroglyphic languages of the

---

[44] Madeleine L'Engle, *Walking on Water* (Colorado Springs: Waterbrook Press, 2001),51.

[45] Chesterton, *The Everlasting Man*, 13.

[46] Ibid., 28.

[47] Ibid., 32.

Egyptians likely developed from rich imaginations rather than prelinguistic limitations; and the walls of Babylon protecting from nomads attest that early man preferred settlement to wandering. Neither did morality or even the family evolve, but instead it is "round the family [that] do indeed gather the sanctities that separate men from bees," sanctities such as decency, liberty, property and honor; "the dawn of history reveals a humanity already civilized." [48] [49]

Chesterton is just as incisive about the apparent democracy of religions: simply creating a list of founders such as Jesus, Mohammed, Buddha and Confucius confuses how different each one was. Instead, Chesteron proposes such categories as God, gods, demons, and philosophers by which to classify faiths and philosophies. The idea of a single God is often behind religions, however polytheistic: that a religion might hold that "every great thing grows from a seed," Chesterton reminds us that "they seem to forget that every seed comes from a tree;" even Confucianism, not intended as a religion, ends up as

---

[48] Chesterton, *The Everlasting Man*, 47.

[49] Ibid., 50.

"a vague theism" replacing "God" with "Heaven." [50][51] Mythologies are often tied to the worship of localities, such as a particular forest or mountain, though otherwise "Mythology is a search" and "man found it natural to worship; even natural to worship unnatural things." [52] [53] Mythologies and religions often turned daydreams into nightmares, as cannibalism and human sacrifice plagued religions from the Old World to the New. Rome's courageous victory against the onslaught of Carthage and Hannibal ('Hanniba'al' translated as 'grace of Ba'al,' the god Moloch transported from Tyre and Sidon which demanded regular child sacrifice), amounted to a victory from "the simultaneous fury [of] the one God in Palestine and the guardians of all the household gods in Rome."[54] The religions of Rome and the Mediterranean, however hearth - and family - oriented they might be at times, offered a more humane face to paganism than did Carthage and Moloch. But Rome's religions had become exhausted:

---

[50] Chesterton, *The Everlasting Man,* 82.

[51] Ibid., 84.

[52] Ibid., 107.

[53] Ibid., 106.

[54] Ibid., 119.

There comes a time in the routine of an ordered civilization when the man is tired of playing at mythology and pretending that a tree is a maiden or that the moon made love to a man . . . Men seek stranger things . . . to stimulate their jaded sense. They seek after mad oriental religions for the same reason. They try to stab their nerves to life.[55]

The specter of Eastern religions did not offer anything better. These were most often philosophies rather than religions, with Confucius coming close to history's first "Philosopher King" (otherwise advocated by Plato; Confucius inspired). The Egyptian King Akenahton achieved that honor, as he replaced Egypt's pantheon of gods with but a single entity, the Sun. Conceiving of God in a circle figure, in fact, symbolized later Asian religious philosophies remarkably well, Chesterton observes, such as with the Asian penchant for viewing life as a cycle, as exemplified in the Wheel of Buddha. This wheel, represented as a swastika, symbolizes for Chesterton nothing but the spinning of a broken cross. At its limit, a circle, it epitomizes "the mind of Asia . . . a round O . . . the great Asiatic symbol of a serpent with its tail in its mouth" striving to

---

[55] Chesterton, *The Everlasting Man*, 155.

represent everything, yet in fact showing how devours itself into nothing.[56] Only the cross, an intersection of sorts, of the eternal God with the external world (dismissed by the Buddha), can break the circle, Chesterton claims. Given the self-renunciation at the heart of Buddhism, Chesterton declares it a "wheel, caught up in a sort of cosmic rotation of which the hollow hub is really nothing."[57] Such philosophizing overly simplifies the matter:

> The temptation of the philosophers is simplicity rather than subtlety. They are always attracted by insane simplifications . . . [that] everything is a dream and a delusion and there is nothing outside the ego. Another is that all things recur; another which is said to be Buddhist and is certainly Oriental, is the idea that what is the matter with us is our creation, in the sense of our coloured differentiation and personality, and that nothing will be well till we are again melted into one unity. By this theory, in short, the Creation was the Fall.[58]

---

[56] Chesterton, *The Everlasting Man,* 129.

[57] Ibid., 126.

[58] Ibid., 131.

Of Hindu thought, Chesterton states

> Gods as well as men are only the dreams of
> Brahma; and will perish when Brahma
> wakes. There is indeed something of the
> soul of Asia which is less sane than the
> soul of Christendom. We should call it
> despair, even if they call it peace.[59]

From *Man in the Cave* to *God in the Cave*: Last And First Christmases

But such despair, paralleling the exhausting of Mediterannean paganism, was answered by another man in a cave, the baby Jesus. Instead of Moloch and Ba'al which had different ideas about babies, the Christian faith presents a startling and novel picture of God: "a picture of a mother and a baby" attendant with "some hint of mercy and softening about the mere mention of the dreadful name of God."[60] Such an image, Chesterton declares, makes growing up Christian so much different from growing up Jewish, Islamic, or even agnostic. Born as an outcast, homeless, and under the hills, "Christ was not only born on the level of the world, but even

---

[59] Chesterton, *The Everlasting Man*, 93.

[60] Ibid., 165.

lower than the world."[61] Implications of duties
toward the poor, outcast, and even slaves were
immediately altered; the exhausted worship of
nature found its answer in a cave, which held more
answers than the "transcendentalism of Plato or the
orientalism of Pythagoras," a cave that was "a place
of dreams come true" so that "since that hour no
mythologies have been made in the world [as]
mythology is a search."[62]

Chesterton continues *The Everlasting Man* for
nearly another hundred pages, but his work was
essentially finished at this point. Christ's birth "had
risen out of the ground to wreck the heaven and
earth of heathenism," engulfing the philosophy,
poetry and even common sense of other systems. [63]
In Chestertonian style, paradoxes abound: "It
proclaims peace on earth and never forgets why
there was war in heaven," and our image of Christ as
meek and mild absolutely misses the voice of one
who says to demons "Hold thy peace and come out
of him," answering Pi's objections to a humble but

---

[61] Chesterton, *The Everlasting Man,* 167.

[62] Ibid., 169.

[63] Ibid., 176.

apparently fight-less Jesus.[64] All competitors fall
short:

> Buddhism may profess to be equally
> mystical; it does not even profess to be
> equally military. Islam may profess to be
> equally military; it does not even profess
> to be equally metaphysical and subtle.
> Confucianism may profess to satisfy the
> need of the philosopher for order and
> reason; it does not even profess the need of
> the mystics for miracle and sacrament
> and consecration of concrete things... No
> other birth of a god or childhood sage
> seems to us to be Christmas or anything
> like Christmas.[65]

The *story* of Christ and Christmas speaks to the
soul as other systems and religions cannot. From
Buddha's wheel to Akhen Aten's sun to Pythagoras
and his mystical idea of "number" to Confucius and
his "religion of routine, there is not one of them
which does not in some sin against the soul of a story
. . . the ordeal of the free man."[66] Whether by
fatalism, indifference, skepticism or materialism,
they miss that "there is a human story; and that

---

[64] Chesterton, *The Everlasting Man,* 178.

[65] Ibid., 178.

[66] Ibid., 240.

there is such a thing as the divine story which is also a human story."[67] That story is a romance, however divine, of God and man, and set within the structure of a family. Just as human virtues of even the first cavemen could be found in the family, so does the Christmas story take place in not just an Earthly trinity of a family, Father, Mother and child, but in a divine family, of Father, Son and Holy Spirit.

Holiday romances, even those of the *Hallmark* Christmas season romances, in some sense capture what Chesterton otherwise terms *The Romance of Orthodoxy*.[68] The 2019 holiday season film release, *Last Christmas*, illustrates: Tom's frequent advice to Kate to "look up" augments the message of giving one's heart away in love, and reinforces Chesterton's claim that it was in a family, built on love, where our notions of love and the virtues first arose. The George Michael soundtrack paid homage to many of the themes found in *Life of Pi*, *Wrinkle in Time* and in Chesterton. In "Praying for Time," Michael acknowledges our divine origin, which leads him to long for justice and a God to enforce it:

---

[67] Chesterton, *The Everlasting Man,* 240.

[68] This is the title of Chapter 8 of his *Orthodoxy*, the chapter from which most of his discussion on world religions in that book can be found.

This is the year of the hungry man ...

'Cause God's stopped keeping score ...

He can't come back

'Cause he has no children to come back for

It's hard to love there's so much to hate.[69]

Michael flashes a germ of faith in finding an enduring love in the soundtrack's next song, "You Gotta Have Faith." But the song "Wake Me Up Before You Go-Go" best evokes Chesterton's argument, however subtly. But the waking is not from some Eastern notion of life as a dream, nor the awakening of Brahman, or even the rising of Akhenaton's sun which ushered in abstract philosophy. Instead, the waking has a *divine* rhythm and the relish of new life invoked by a sunrise, which Chesterton describes with:

> A child kicks his legs rhythmically through excess, not absence, of life. Because children have abounding vitality,

---

[69] George Michael, *Praying for Time* (Sony Music Entertainment UK Limited, 2017).

because they are in spirit fierce and free, therefore they want things repeated and unchanged. The always say "Do it again" and the grown-up person does it again until he is nearly exhausted. For grown up people are not strong enough to exult in monotony. But perhaps God is strong enough to exult in monotony. It is possible that God says every morning "Do it again" to the sun; and every evening "Do it again" to the moon. It may not be automatic necessity that makes all daisies alike; it may be that God makes every daisy separately, but has never got tired of making them. It may be that He has the eternal appetite of infancy; for we have sinned and grown old, and our Father is younger than we. The repetition in Nature may not be a mere recurrence; it may be a theatrical encore.[70]

But the circular figure of the sun ultimately gives way to a sketch of the round face of a loving mother, and of a Son.

Merry Christmas.

---

[70] G.K. Chesterton, *Orthodoxy*, 44.

FRANCES CHESTERTON AND CHRISTMAS

Nancy Carpenter Brown

Frances Chesterton, wife of famous British author and Christian apologist G.K. Chesterton, was obsessed with Christmas. Obsessed.

Frances had a nativity set up in every room, each one unique in size, shape, and style. She collected miniature ornaments and kept them on display all year round. She wrote Christmas plays, spending months writing, planning, sewing costumes and painting sets. Her poetry centered on a Christmas theme and each year she wrote a new poem to be included in the family Christmas card that she sent out to all of their friends.

Why? What was it about Christmas that drew Frances?

Frances Alice Blogg grew up in a Victorian middle class household that was perhaps troubled. Her mother suffered from depression, her father may have had affairs. George Blogg died of a heart attack at the youthful age of 41, when Frances was just fourteen. Her broken home only continued to break more as time went on: her beloved sister Gertrude died in a bicycle accident, and her brother committed suicide. When she met and married Gilbert Keith Chesterton, she may have thought her life was complete. Her broken family was once again whole.

But she continued to experience brokenness. The early years of her marriage passed, and no babies came along. The couple saw several doctors, and Frances had operations, but nothing cured the problem. And the couple failed to do the one thing Frances had wanted more than anything: to have a whole family. And what she experienced instead was more brokenness.

However, their infertility did not overwhelm them. Gilbert and Frances were a strong couple, they had faith, and they believed God had a plan for their lives. They made a decision to welcome all children, and this extended to the Christ Child — or perhaps instead the Christ Child inspired them.

From the moment they discovered that they could no longer hope to have biological children, Gilbert and Frances seem to have made a pact. They would welcome children into their homes and hearts as often as they could. When choosing the railway car when they traveled, they chose the car with the most children. If families came over to visit, they made a point to talk to the children and made sure they felt welcomed.

At first, the couple had one nativity set, which they set up each Christmas. But during their early travels, Frances came upon another nativity set she loved, and when she got it home, she set it up immediately. From then on, whenever she saw a set she liked, she bought it and set it up in another room.

And as she looked at that nativity, with tiny little baby Jesus, she began to contemplate that wintry scene. She used her imagination to wonder what it would be like to hold the Christ Child? What if she touched his tiny hand? What if she felt the ox and ass breathing in the stable? What if she saw Mary and Joseph?

And as she thought about these things, and more, she began composing poetry. How far is it to Bethlehem? She wondered, perhaps even looking on a map. But then she thought of another layer to that question. How far is it for me to get to the Holy Family? Can I have a holy family...even if I don't have children? What kind of family do I have if I invite Jesus — in the hidden disguise of my neighbors, nieces and nephews — into my family?

Frances and Gilbert wondered what it would be like to adopt a baby. Frances's sister Ethel lived nearby and had five children, and two of the girls were particularly close to their Auntie Frances and Uncle Chestnut. Should they adopt them? The idea was contemplated, and then dropped. The girls were already family.

During this time, Frances wrote a lovely Christmas play called *The Christmas Gift*, in which the father, missing in the First World War, finally returns home with a foundling in his arms. The parents already have three children, but the mother takes the baby in as her own. "Is he the Christ Child?" asks one of her children. "Oh darling, who can tell?" Frances has the mother answer. She reminds us that every child is an image of the Baby Jesus, and any baby just might be the Holy Child.

Frances invited the children visiting her home to play games, cards, or sit and talk while sipping tea. The teen girls noted that Frances was a good listener and particularly helpful to them when they entered adolescence. But she was also good at making treasure hunts for the smaller ones. And then she loved plays and pageants. In a cupboard in the morning room of their home, the Chestertons had boxes and boxes of fabric and costumes, and wigs and props of all sorts. Putting on a play or dressing up to spontaneously perform some bits from Shakespeare were common activities at the Chesterton home. Frances got all the children involved, painting sets and hammering boxes for tables. The Chesterton home had an interesting design element — in the living room was an area raised up a step, that had a curtain across it that could completely close. This area was made for putting on plays right in the living room. One small step, and you were on center stage.

Another happy place at the Chesterton home was the garden. Frances poured over the gardening and seed catalogs that came to the house, picturing the plants and how they would look in the garden. She loved planning out the order of the colors and planting tall spiky plants like foxglove, delphiniums and hollyhocks. Gilbert would give tours through the garden making up names for all the flowers, saying things like "Look, that one's monk's breath. This here is Bishop's Bigamy," and so forth. He said these words so seriously that most people didn't catch that he was joking. Frances encouraged the children to pick bouquets and arrange them in a vase, and as they arranged, they talked about life. The children played hide-and-seek with each other and fetch with the dog. The Chestertons had a slew of pets, including a donkey for the children to pet.

There's a saying that is sometimes repeated, although it seems more in the category of legend since there's never a source, that is this: Frances says to Gilbert, "Darling, why don't you write more about God?" as if she's critical of Gilbert's writing in the journals of the day. "My love," Gilbert supposedly says, "that's all I do write about."

As I said this may have never happened, and I suppose one reason I don't like it is because it puts Frances in a bad light. But when I do think about if this conversation ever did take place, I like to think that it's a little joke between Gilbert and Frances. This couple talked about God together and they prayed together. And Frances often read over Gilbert's essays and made small corrections in spelling and grammar (for which she jokingly charged him a penny per correction), so she knows exactly what his essays are about and how he thinks about God. So I like to think she's joking when she asks why he doesn't write *more* about God. How can you write more about God when everything you write *is* about God?

Gilbert and Frances were obsessed by Christmas, because both of them loved the Christ Child—and because they loved children. Their poetry, plays and home decoration all reflected this; but more than that, their lives reflected this. Let us love the Christ

Child and all the children that ever come into our lives, whether biologically or otherwise—as they both demonstrated.

Chesterton as Poet:
The Wise Men

G.K. Chesterton

Step softly, under snow or rain,
　To find the place where men can pray;
The way is all so very plain
　That we may lose the way.

Oh, we have learnt to peer and pore
　On tortured puzzles from our youth,
We know all the labyrinthine lore,
We are the three wise men of yore,
　And we know all things but truth.

We have gone round and round the hill
　And lost the wood among the trees,
And learnt long names for every ill,
And serve the made gods, naming still
　The furies the Eumenides.

The gods of violence took the veil
　Of vision and philosophy,

The Serpent that brought all men bale,
He bites his own accursed tail,
  And calls himself Eternity.

Go humbly ... it has hailed and snowed...
  With voices low and lanterns lit;
So very simple is the road,
  That we may stray from it.

The world grows terrible and white,
  And blinding white the breaking day;
We walk bewildered in the light,
For something is too large for sight,
  And something much too plain to say.

The Child that was ere worlds begun
  (... We need but walk a little way,
We need but see a latch undone...)
The Child that played with moon and sun
  Is playing with a little hay.

The house from which the heavens are fed,
  The old strange house that is our own,
Where trick of words are never said,
And Mercy is as plain as bread,
  And Honour is as hard as stone.

Go humbly, humble are the skies,
  And low and large and fierce the Star;
So very near the Manger lies
  That we may travel far.

Hark! Laughter like a lion wakes
  To roar to the resounding plain.
And the whole heaven shouts and shakes,
For God Himself is born again,
And we are little children walking
  Through the snow and rain.

Resources

To Connect with An Unexpected Journal

An Unexpected Journal is published quarterly; however, the conversation does not end. Join us on social media for discussion with the authors weekly:

An Unexpected Journal online:
http://anunexpectedjournal.com

On Facebook:
https://www.facebook.com/anunexpectedjournal/

On Twitter: https://twitter.com/anujournal

On Instagram:
https://www.instagram.com/anujournal/

On Pinterest:
https://www.pinterest.com/anunexpectedjournal/

Comments and feedback can be submitted at
http://anunexpectedjournal.com/contact/
Be sure to sign up for our newsletter for announcements on new editions and events near you: http://anunexpectedjournal.com/newsletter

TO READ MORE

When discussing theology, or philosophy, or literature, or art, one is stepping into and taking part of a larger conversation that has been taking place for centuries. Each essay within the journal contains not only the thoughts of the individual author, but draws upon works and thinkers of the past. It is our hope that the writing not only engages your interest in the specific essay topic, but that you join us in the Great Conversation.

To read more, please visit http://anunexpectedjournal.com/resources/ for a list of the works cited within the essays of the journal.

SUBSCRIBE

Yearly subscriptions to *An Unexpected Journal* are available through our web site. Please visit http://anunexpectedjournal.com/subscribe for more information. For bulk pricing, events, or speaking requests, please send an email to anunexpectedjournal@gmail.com.

About An Unexpected Journal

The Inspiration

J. R. R. Tolkien and C. S. Lewis, both members of The Inklings writers group, are well-known for their fiction embedded with Christian themes. These fantasy writers, who were also philosophers and teachers, understood the important role imagination plays in both exercising and expanding the faculties of the mind as well as the development of faith.

Beyond the parables of Jesus, their works are the gold standard for imaginative apologetics. The title, *An Unexpected Journal*, is a nod to the work to which Tolkien devoted much of his life, *The Lord of the Rings*.

Our Story

An Unexpected Journal is the endeavor of a merry band of Houston Baptist University Master of Arts in Apologetics students and alumni. What began as simply a Facebook post on November 1, 2017 wishing that there was an outlet for imaginative apologetics quickly organized by the end of the year into a very real and very exciting quarterly publication.

Our Mission

An Unexpected Journal seeks to demonstrate the truth of Christianity through both reason and the imagination to engage the culture from a Christian worldview.

OUR CONTRIBUTORS

Nancy Carpenter Brown
www.nancy-brown.com

Brown is the author of The Woman Who Was Chesterton, a biography of Frances Chesterton, wife of British Journalist G.K. Chesterton

Donald W. Catchings, Jr.
www.donaldwcatchingsjr.com

Donald W. Catchings, Jr. is Founder and Board Chair of Street Light Inc. and Pastor of The True Light Church in Conroe, Texas since 2009. Donald graduated from Liberty University in 2018 with a Bachelor of Science in Biblical and Educational Studies. He is currently enrolled in Houston Baptist University's Apologetics program. As a writer, Donald regularly contributes to 'An Unexpected Journal.' Also, Donald will be releasing a book of poetry and reflection on The Lion, the Witch and the Wardrobe in Spring 2020 through Wipf and Stock.

Mark D. Linville

Mark D. Linville holds a PhD in philosophy from the University of Wisconsin-Madison and is Senior Research Fellow and Philosophy Fellow for the PhD Program in the Humanities at Faulkner University.

Seth Myers
www.narnianfrodo.com

Seth Myers completed his MA in Cultural Apologetics from Houston Baptist University in 2017. As a power systems engineer, he has been involved with transformer diagnostics and rural electrification projects by partnering with NGOs in West Africa. A volunteer with international students through local churches, he enjoys conversations with friends from all cultures. He considers himself rich in friendships across time and space, including but not limited to C.S. Lewis, J.R.R. Tolkien, Bede the Venerable, Augustine, Ravi Zacharias & friends, and many student friends (chess-playing when possible, but not required) typically from throughout Asia. He has recently begun taking online courses in Faulkner University's Doctor of Humanities program.

Joseph Pearce
www.Jpearce.co

A native of England, Joseph Pearce is Director of Book Publishing at the Augustine Institute, and editor of the St. Austin Review (www.staustinreview.org), editor of Faith & Culture (www.faithandculture.com), series editor of the Ignatius Critical Editions (www.ignatiuscriticaleditions.com), senior instructor with Homeschool Connections (www.homeschoolconnectionsonline.com), and senior contributor at the Imaginative Conservative. His personal website is jpearce.co.

Zachary Schmoll
www.rebuildinghollin.com

Zak Schmoll is the founder of Entering the Public Square (www.enteringthepublicsquare.com), a blog founded on the sincere belief that every Christian should understand the importance of discussing Christianity in the marketplace of ideas. He earned his MA in Apologetics at Houston Baptist University and is currently a PhD student in Humanities at Faulkner University. His work has been featured on several websites including The Federalist, the Public Discourse and the Fourth World Journal.

Melissa Cain Travis
www.melissatravis.com

Melissa serves as an Assistant Professor of Christian Apologetics at Houston Baptist University, where she teaches courses in philosophical apologetics and the intersection of science and Christianity. She is the author of Science and the Mind of the Maker: What the Conversation Between Faith and Science Reveals About God and is on the Contributing Writers team for Christian Research Journal. She holds a PhD in Humanities with a philosophy concentration and a master's in Science and Religion. Her research interests include Johannes Kepler, the history of scientific thought, and philosophy of mind.

Rebekah Valerius
www.alongthebeam.com

Rebekah Valerius holds a M.A. in Cultural Apologetics from Houston Baptist University and is part of the Mama Bear Apologetics Ministry team (www.mamabearapologetics.com). She is a wife and homeschooling mother of two. You can see more of her writing at www.alongthebeam.com.

Michael Ward
www.michaelward.net

Michael Ward is Professor of Apologetics at Houston Baptist University and Senior Research Fellow at Blackfriars Hall, University of Oxford. He is the author of Planet Narnia: The Seven Heavens in the Imagination of C.S. Lewis (Oxford University Press) and co-editor of The Cambridge Companion to C.S. Lewis (Cambridge University Press). From 2015-2020 he was the Chairman of the Trustees of the G.K. Chesterton Library, Oxford, a world-class collection of Chestertoniana, which is now located at the London campus of the University of Notre Dame.

Clark Weidner

www.thesolidfaith.com

Clark Weidner is the founder of Solid Faith: A Podcast, blog, vlog, and Christian apologetics website. He is currently pursuing a Masters degree in Cultural Apologetics from Houston Baptist University. He holds a blue belt in jiu jitsu and plenty of scars from years of skateboarding. He met his wife Amber in a Lord of the Rings book club and now they have a dog named Thanos (due to their love of comics).

Shawn White

Shawn White has an M.A. in Christian Apologetics from Biola University and is currently pursuing a Ph.D. at Faulkner University studying Philosophy of Humanities. His academic interests include G.K. Chesterton and Chesterton's writings on gratitude, wonder, and humility. His non-academic interests include having a wife, having a dog, and playing board games.

THOUGHTS FROM A FELLOW TRAVELER

By Jack Tollers

If you aren't a Christian and have somehow gotten to the point where you are reading this, then I must warn you about the pebble in your shoe. For that is what it is like to be around Christians who discuss things together, whether or not they are "Christian kinds of things" that are discussed. At a certain point you will notice something about their point of view, something in their underlying assumptions, and to be honest when you do it will become quite annoying.

That is the pebble I was referring to.

But it gets worse.

Maybe it is not your fault that you happen to be reading this, and you've done a pretty good job milling about life without bumping into too much of this sort of Christian stuff. It could be the case that you haven't really made a conscious effort to avoid Christianity, but chances are (if you are reading this) that is going to change. Somewhere along the line, perhaps even in the course of reading this journal, even, a pebble has worked its way into your shoe, and eventually the pebble will have to be dealt with.

It's not my job to tell you what it is. (I don't really know what "it" is in your case. All I know is that when the pebble got into my shoe, it got to the point where I couldn't walk much further without annoying my heel something terrible.) What I can do is suggest to you something that would have helped me if I had come across it in the back of some obscure journal: The pebble does not exist for itself. The pebble makes you stop and deal with the pebble. Stopping to deal with the pebble leads to thinking about your shoe. Then you start thinking about how much further up the trail you'd be if it weren't for that blasted pebble, which leads to thoughts about the trail itself and the path you're walking . . . and so on.

A particular Christian, or a particular thought expressed by a Christian, or perhaps just the particular quality you meet in places and things of Christian origin will eventually function to put you in mind of something beyond or behind themselves. I say something because I'm trying to be non-partisan, but really I mean someone. Because at some point, the context for these thoughts will change to an awareness that this Christ person has been behind all of it.

When this moment comes, avoid mistaking Jesus for the pebble in your shoe. (If you do, it won't be long before another pebble gets in there and starts the whole thing off again. It took me years to figure that out.) Instead, consider the possibility that he is more like the path than the pebble. He said as much himself when he told Thomas, "I am the way, the truth and the life. No man comes to the Father except by me."

The truth aspect of Jesus' claim is, of course, exclusive. But there is more to his self disclosure. The other terms, "the way" and "the life" point us beyond a mere static assertion of fact or a single point of view toward a dynamic process of relational involvement. The pursuit of truth leads to knowing Jesus (if he indeed is truth incarnate). Thus, just as travelers come to know a country by living in it and exploring it, so people will grow in their knowledge of Truth as they make their way through life, the path itself bringing us in proximity to Jesus.

Such a journey, so conceived, is bound to take a person through some interesting experiences, and to unexpected places. Once the pebble is out of the shoe.

> All the way to heaven is heaven for he said,
> "I am the way" — St. Catherine of Sienna

> "And ye shall seek me, and find me, when ye shall search for me with all your heart."
> —Jeremiah 29:13

Made in the USA
Lexington, KY
12 December 2019